Doing the Impossible

Neil E. Jackson, Jr.

DOING THE IMPOSSIBLE

BROADMAN PRESS
Nashville, Tennessee

© Copyright 1985 • Broadman Press
All rights reserved
4250-21
ISBN Number: 0-8054-5021-1

All Scripture quotations are from the King
James Version of the Holy Bible.

Dewey Decimal Classification: 158
Subject Headings: PSYCHOLOGY, APPLIED //
MOTIVATION (PSYCHOLOGY)
Library of Congress Catalog Card Number: 85-5266
Printed in the United States of America

Library of Congress Cataloging in Publication Data

Jackson, Neil E.
    Doing the impossible.

    1. Conduct of life.   2. Christian life—1960-
3. Goal (Psychology)   4. Motivation (Psychology)
I. Title.
BJ1581.2.J33   1985   248.4′86132   85-5266
ISBN 0-8054-5021-1

Dedication

To "Mom" and "Pop" (Esta and Neil) who by their lives gave me visions of basic life principles

To "Pop" who taught me to "finish the job"

To "Mom" who doesn't know the meaning of the word *can't*

My heartfelt thanks and love

Neil, Jr.

Foreword

If you are looking for a book to help you develop the leadership quality of motivation, *Doing the Impossible* by Neil E. Jackson, Jr., is just such a resource.

Jackson deals with motivation through integrity, enthusiasm, and practical expertise. He presents motivation as a vital life dimension.

Jackson makes the point that a person must first motivate himself in order to motivate others. The bedrock principle of spiritual motivation is outlined as foundational. Add to that the motivating characteristics of key activities, and the motivation can be a reality for every leader.

Suggestions for motivating others are presented in large chunks and with specific details. The broad dimension of motivation with a high sense of purpose sets the framework for the book. Then Jackson presents myriads of motivational ideas gleaned from a lifetime of practical experience and diligent study. One new idea may be worth more than the price of the book.

Christian leaders want to work together effectively, with dreams and goals that shape the future. If you, like the apostle Paul, "press toward the mark," this book is for you. May our Lord give you success in your role as motivator.

LLOYD ELDER, President
The Sunday School Board
of the Southern Baptist
Convention

Introduction

Doing the Impossible is a "how-to" book. It is also a "can-do" book. Neil Jackson has done it again! He has given us a book which has been born from his own life experiences, providing practical help and self-motivation. It is literally laced with life experiences. Neil Jackson clearly sees and conveys the absolute necessity of self-acceptance. He talks about the attitude and the value of "what we think about."

Neil comes across not only as a positive thinker, but also as one who sees that quality is essential and biblical. In fact, he wisely uses the Scriptures as a basis for his ideas and concepts throughout the book. This book gives keen insight into how persons are motivated.

He begins with the fundamental truth that each person is important and has immeasurable potential. Then he builds upon that basic fact and shows how to motivate people. Again, by using personal experiences and innovative ideas, Neil provides a potpourri of ways to motivate persons.

If you want a sound, practical, helpful book, this book is it! Pastors, staff members, Sunday School directors, and other laypersons will find invaluable and usable material within these pages.

HARRY PILAND, Secretary
Sunday School Department
BSSB

Contents

God Specializes in . . .
The Impossible!

"Is any thing too hard for the Lord?" (Gen. 18:14).

"If ye have faith as a grain of mustard seed, ye shall say unto this mountain, Remove hence to yonder place; and it shall remove; and nothing shall be impossible unto you" (Matt. 17:20).

"For with God nothing shall be impossible" (Luke 1:37).

The Author's Page

My desire for you is: as you read, may you discover the dynamic potential which lies within you.

As a butterfly—bursting forth from its cocoon, stretching its wings and discovering it is no longer a caterpillar but a creature of beauty which soars to heights that seemed impossible on winds carrying it to places never before seen—you, yes *you,* have capabilities never before released or tapped. Whatever you can envision in your mind and genuinely believe, you can be. You can do what you set your heart and mind to do.

You are already headed toward achievement. No doubt thoughts of success have already raced through your brain. You are a winner. Winners never really lose; losers never really win.

A winner wrote in Philippians 4:13: "I can do all things through Christ which strengtheneth me."

"I can do . . . I can do . . . I can do." Say it out loud so you can hear yourself. I CAN DO! From time to time when you are alone, repeat it aloud—shout it, sing it, write it. I CAN DO! I CAN DO!

You are in the process of removing yourself from the cocoon of nonentity into the fresh air and sunlight of victorious living! Enjoy it!

NEIL E. JACKSON, JR.

PART I.
How to Motivate Yourself

Working on Attitude

This book is primarily written to Christians and has considerable Scripture used throughout. However, the principles can be used by anyone, and it would not be out of order for a nonbeliever to look in the Scriptures as proof texts to the ideas and ideals set forth in the Word of God. It may possibly cause non-Christians to accept Christ as their personal Savior. What a grand, glorious goal that would be for the reader to attain.

The Scriptures are filled with passages that deal with the concept of positive thinking. One verse already used is Philippians 4:13: "I can do all things through Christ which strengtheneth me." I can do, I can do, I can do.

The believer would first ask himself the question, "What would Christ have me do? It may be to teach a Sunday School class or sing in the choir, be a music director, a pianist, a preacher, a missionary. There are hundreds of tasks a person could do for the glory of God. But many people have never stopped long enough to ask, "Lord, what wouldest thou have me to do?"

Once a person knows the direction God has for his/her life, they can claim other Scripture verses in order to attain the goal God has given them. For example, in Matthew 17:20: "If you have faith as a grain of mustard seed, you shall say unto this mountain, Remove hence to yonder place; and it shall remove and nothing shall be impossible unto you."

In Mark 11:23 it says "That whosoever shall say unto this mountain, Be thou removed and be thou cast into the sea; and shall not doubt in his heart, but shall believe that those things which he saith shall come to pass; he shall have whatsoever he saith." Luke 17:6 declares: "If ye had faith as a grain of mustard seed, ye might say unto this sycamore tree, Be thou plucked up by the root, and be thou planted in the sea, and it should obey you."

These verses deal with one's faith in God and, I believe, faith in oneself. All too often the problem is we will take a passage of Scripture like this and give a literal application. Many assume, "Since I have no mountains to move or trees in the way, this must not apply to me." However, my personal understanding of these passages refers to when God calls you to do a work, and the obstacles loom as large as a mountain, or what keeps you from accomplishing a task is like a sycamore tree in your pathway. You say it's impossible; it can't be done.

God is trying to tell us: If we have faith in Him and He calls us to do a work, we are to assume the task, call upon Him for strength and guidance, and He will help us meet the obstacle—to find a way around it, through it, above it, alongside of it, or literally to blast it out of the way and have it removed. "For with God nothing shall be impossible" (Lk. 1:37). Another Scripture that strengthens this concept is, "For as he thinketh in his heart, so is he" (Prov. 23:7).

Therefore, the person that constantly thinks "I can do," and has the faith to believe that what he wants to accomplish can be accomplished, will have accomplishments.

You can do whatever you want to do if you want to do

it badly enough. Instead of building mind-set and ima,
to think of impossibility, build a mind-set to work on
solving the problems that come your way, keeping in mind
that each problem is a possibility. Each possibility can be
a rewarding stepping stone to the next task that comes
before you. Success comes as stepping stones over obstacles to the desired goal in a daily faith in God and self.

How to Build Faith in Yourself

Start with small goals that can be attained. As you
attain the small goals, create new and bigger ones. Make
each new goal a little more difficult, which will cause you
to stretch yourself beyond what you accomplished on the
last goal.

For example, take a deep breath, inhaling as much as
you can. Hold it to the count of five, inhale again, bringing
in more air without exhaling the first breath. Count to five.
Now exhale. You see, you thought when you took the first
breath that your lungs were full, but you discovered, as
you held your breath and attempted again, you were able
to take in more air. As you held your breath and inhaled
again, you were made aware that you could inhale far
more air than thought possible.

Many times when we attempt to accomplish a goal, we
think we've given our all. No matter what you have already attained, you discover there is always a capacity for
more.

The Be-Attitude of Positive Thinking

In the book of Matthew (5:3-12) is the section called
"The Beatitudes." The word *beatitude* comes from the
root word which means *blessed* or *happy*.

You will notice each beatitude starts with the word
"blessed."

- "Blessed are the poor . . ."
- "Blessed are they that mourn . . ."
- "Blessed are the meek . . ."
- And so forth. The word *blessed* means happy.

Allow me the privilege of stretching your mind a little and doing a play on words. Change the spelling of the word *Beatitude* slightly to *Beattitude*. It is pronounced the same, but I think it can have a deeper, fuller, broader meaning to each of us personally.

Beattitude Be-attitude. Whatever your attitude is, that is what *you* are going to be.

- A positive attitude produces positive results.
- A negative attitude produces negative results.
- A sweet attitude produces a sweet relationship.
- A sour attitude produces poor relationships.
- A winning attitude produces a winner.
- A losing attitude produces a loser.
- A loving attitude produces love.
- A hateful attitude produces *hate, heartache,* and *hives!*

If we take this attitudinal change to heart, we truly can be happy in whatever we are doing. As the apostle Paul put it, "In whatsoever state I am [I have learned] therewith to be content" (Phil. 4:11). Attitude controls the emotions and either gives acceptability to the situation or a high level of frustration and emotional strain.

You are becoming what you think about. The big question is: What do you think about and how do you think about it? Positive or negative?

A certain person was attempting to go to the top of Pike's Peak in Colorado. (Incidentally, I'm told there are three ways to go to the top: drive, take a tram car, or walk.)

This person was attempting to walk to the top. There are places to stop along the way to sit, rest, and view the scenery. At about the third or fourth level this person had stopped to sit and rest. Breathing heavily and gasping for air he remarked to a person nearby: "It must be the *attitude* that keeps me from going any higher." What he meant to say was the *altitude,* but it came out *attitude.* The statement "attitude" was probably true, for the person had stopped, and this was what kept him from going any higher. Our attitude either helps us reach goals and higher planes of life or causes us to stop at lower levels of existence.

Our attitude should be like the hymn, "I'm pressing on the upward way,/New heights I'm gaining ev'ry day./Still praying as I onward bound, 'Lord lead me on to higher ground.'"

In the Beatitudes in Matthew 5, verse 1, says, "He [Jesus] went up into a mountain: . . . and his disciples came unto him." The previous chapter tells of the "multitudes" following Jesus for the "loaves and fishes." Notice that the multitudes stopped climbing when the going got tough. To follow Jesus closely and to reach some goals in life, one will have to climb some mountains, go to higher altitudes, exert effort and energy, and change attitudes to reach higher altitudes. We will need to develop a closer relationship with Christ and a deeper determination within ourselves.

Higher ground is a place for the selected few, but the rewards are worth it all.

What are the benefits or rewards for the "higher" or goal-oriented life?

At higher altitudes the view is more inclusive (insights,

To reach higher Altitudes we have to change our Attitude

perceptions, and broadened vision of awareness are keener), at higher altitudes the air is cleaner and fresher (your
leadership will possess a freshness and newness that will
draw people to you).

At higher altitudes the air is cooler (under pressure
your ability to stay cool will increase).

At higher altitudes your circulation improves, blood
flows to the brain faster (your mind will think positive
ideas and be more creative than before). Negativism and
negative people will fall away from you (the multitudes).
. . . .

At higher altitudes pollution diminishes (the pollution
of the world has less attraction and hold on you). The
negative attitudes become less, and thoughts of impossibility dilute themselves and disappear. Success brings satisfaction, and satisfaction gives more drive.

At higher altitudes you will see things you never saw
before, since sights and insights become sharper. Christ
and His purpose for your life will be more evident than
ever before. Other talents and gifts you possess will surface. Early in life, writing was not one of my gifts. But as
I "climbed higher" the gift of writing came to the surface.

Ask yourself, "What is my altitude in relation to myself
and others?

"What do I want to be? Do I want to be what I am
becoming? Am I happy at what I am becoming and am
presently doing?"

"Blessed are ye" or happy are you when your "Be-
Attitude" is right.

What does it take to be happy? It may take change—

- Change of attitude
- Change of altitude
- Change of mind-set

- Change of life-style
- Change of job
- Change of habits
- Change of goals
- Change of many things

When you stop changing, you have stopped. When you have stopped and are doing nothing, remember that nothing is happening. *You* are the one causing nothing to happen, so get moving.

If you are at the point where nothing right seems to be happening, or nothing seems to be happening at all, *you can change.* A born-again, Bible-believing, saint can fully believe in Philippians 4:13, "I can do all things through Christ which strengtheneth me." Say to yourself out loud as you are reading, "I CAN DO, I CAN DO." What do you want to do? Then do it. To many people hearing themselves say these words, "I can do" almost startles them, for it may be the first time in a long time, if ever, they have made the assertion, *I CAN DO.* But remember, with Christ *all* things are possible, and you *can* have a powerful, positive outlook on life. You can have a powerful, positive influence on people you minister to in your Sunday School class, department, church, and your everyday life. Look for possibilities, not problems. Look for potentialities, not pot holes.

God gives everyone of us three things—time, energy, and resources. All of us have the same amount of time while we have it. Each of us has varying levels of energy, but we all have energy, but our resources, people, or money will vary.

Accept Yourself

A problem often arising is: many people find fault with themselves, dwell on their supposed faults, weaknesses, difficulties, problems, and come up with excuses as to why they don't attempt or do certain things. "You know, I have this problem. I'd do certain things if I didn't have this problem!" This is a poor excuse. You know what an excuse is? It's a skin of a reason stuffed full of lies. We need to accept ourselves the way God made us—accept ourselves the way we are, with the personalities we have. And we need to accept ourselves in what may appear to be some physical problem—and then, God willing, we may overcome that problem.

Some things can be changed physically. If you are overweight, there is the possibility of change. Set your mind to do so. There are operations that can be performed to solve some physical problems, such as a facelift or alterations of a nose or a jaw. If this will solve the problem— operate. However, I am reminded of the Scripture which declares, "This one thing I do, forgetting those things which are behind and reaching forth unto those things which are before, I press toward the mark for the prize of the high calling. . . ." (Phil. 3:13-14).

Do not spend time feeling sorry for yourself because of a physical condition that cannot be changed. Self-pity never motivates. Forget the problems you can't solve. Set a goal and go for it.

When I was in high school, I had a schoolmate who was born with only one arm. He wanted to play basketball. It seemed as if there were no way he could ever play. However, his desire was so strong that he practiced continuously. In his sophomore year he made varsity and played all through his high school years. Physical condition did not stop him.

One day I was listening to a multimillionaire, a great motivator, telling how he became successful.

The man's apparent problem was his harelip and a terrible nasal lisp. Speaking to the group, he said, "Everyone has problems of some kind. Everyone has difficulties to overcome. Everyone seems to have impossibilities. Everyone seems to have something standing in his way, keeping him from accomplishing their goal." His statement was, "Forget your problems. Concentrate on a goal. Act as though you have no problems or are not aware of them."

Now keep in mind that this man had a terrible speech impediment and was lisping in a distracting nasal tone. His classic illustration was, in his own vocal sounds, "New tink new dot problems; new don't know what problems are. Loot dat me. Now I dot problems. I dot real problems. Loot dat me, no wat my problems dar?" A long pause and finally he said, I dot flat feet!" The audience caught his message. His big problem was not flat feet. His determination to succeed was greater than any physical handicap. He refused to recognize the real handicap, the speech impediment. Many can conquer or overcome a problem or difficulty. It depends on how we look at it—God made you the way you are for a purpose. Accept how you are, and go on as if the way you are is the "norm."

There is a young evangelist in Memphis, Tennessee, who had cerebral palsy which left him with a dreadful speech impediment. He also walks with a decided limp and impoverished muscle control. I have heard him preach on several occasions, and he is an excellent preacher in spite of his speech impediment and physical difficulties. After one of that preacher's services, a surgeon proudly told him he could perform several operations and make him normal like most folks.

Much to the shock and amazement of the surgeon the indignant young man lispingly replied, "Man new tink I'm cwazzy? Dis is da way God made me. New tink I want to lose my twademark?" He has become so identified and successful in the way he is that to change him would be to lose all he has overcome and gained.

Think positive. Think possibilities. Don't spend time and energy thinking the problems can't be solved. Think of possible ways to solve the problem.

Look for the positive, possible, potential solution.

Edison, when attempting to invent the battery that starts our automobiles, made eighteen thousand experiments before he succeeded. When discovering how to make the light bulb, he made 756 attempts. Someone remarked, "You have failed 756 times." His remark was, "I did not fail, for I know 756 things that will not work."

Trying to accomplish a task which does not come about is not failure, for you learned it would not work the way you tried. Failure comes when you *fail to try*. So keep on trying. Therefore, make the attempt—try. If it does not work, ask yourself, "What do I need to do to change it until it will work?"

Remember, nothing happens unless you *make it* happen.

Stay happy! Remember, the Scripture, "I have learned in whatsoever state I am, therewith to be content" (Phil. 4:11). Therefore, contentment is a state of mind.

"Thou wilt keep him in perfect peace whose mind is stayed on thee" (Isa. 26:3). Peace is a state of mind.

When depressed, learn to look around at other people. You will soon learn you are better off than many people. Remember the gospel song, "Count your blessings, name them one by one:/Count your many blessings, see what God has done."

Depression is a form of selfishness—a person gets to feeling sorry for himself: "Oh, poor me, oh poor me!" That wastes time and energy and does no one any good. May I suggest a helpful biblical word study? Use a Bible concordance, look at all the Scriptures in the Bible on the words: *happy/happiness, joy/peace, content,* and other positive mind-set words. It will change and strengthen your own personal life and outlook.

Living on the Positive Side

A leader, living on the positive side of Christ, can have tremendous influence on those with whom he comes in contact. You ask, how can I live on the positive side of life? Make a note: God never intended for a person to live on the negative side. When one sees a newborn child and watches him grow up through the preschool period, it is fun to see that child assert himself and be a free spirit. It is through training that children are taught to think negatively. Much of their inquisitive, creative nature is suppressed. They constantly hear the words, "You can't do that." "Don't do that." "Stop." "Quit." "Don't go there." "Don't touch," and on goes the list until after a while the children learn, if they are going to get along in life, they had better not be too assertive or creative, or they will suffer the consequences. Therefore, negativism is a learned environmental process.

Let's look at the Bible again and see this passage of Scripture: "As [a man] thinketh in his heart, so is he" (Prov. 23:7).

If you think positively, positive results will occur. If you think negatively, negative things will happen.

Now, Let us think along the lines of church growth.

Pastor, minister of education, Sunday School worker, and church leader, do you have a positive attitude toward church growth—that is, reaching people for Christ, winning the lost, seeing people saved, born again, growing and developing, and in a right relationship with God? Right now, let's take a look at ourselves.

What do you *think* about? How do you think? Do you even think?

Let's ask ourselves several questions that will reveal how positively we think. First of all, what do I think about the way my life is going with my:

(Check one)	*Happy*	*Unhappy*	*No feeling*
• Job		•	
• Home	÷		
• Family	÷		
• Finances			
• Future		•	
• Christian life		♭	
• Friends	–		
• Influence		•	
• Spouse	•		
• Children	◦		
• Retirement		•	
• Business			•
• Love life			◦

All of the statements listed may not necessarily apply to you. However, the majority will. Can you change any of them? Write a statement about what needs to be done to make you happy.

Let's ask ourselves several questions and write a statement about each question.

• What do I think about when my mind is free?

- What is my mind-set toward things in general?
- What involvement do I have toward other people?
- What is my attitude toward life in general?

Write a positive statement that will contain an "action" you can do to effect a change in attitude, life-style, and matters in general. Set a date when you plan to start that action. Set a goal and a completion of that goal or change.

Keeping the Mind Positive

One of the best means of keeping the mind positive is to read books on success such as *Psycho-Cybernetics, Thinking Success, The Power of Positive Thinking, Motivational Ideas for Changing Lives, Success, Motivation, and the Scriptures, How to Win Friends and Influence People,* and others.

Employ the Word of God, preferably on a daily basis. The Scripture says, "Hide the Word of God in your heart that you might not sin against God" (Ps. 119:11, author's words).

"Thou wilt keep him in perfect peace, whose mind is stayed on thee" (Isa. 26:3).

"Set your affections on things above" (Col. 3:2).

"Delight thyself also in the Lord" (Ps. 37:4).

"As [a man] thinketh in his heart, so is he" (Prov. 23:7).

The apostle Paul wrote: "I die daily [to old things]" (1 Cor. 15:31).

He also said: "Forgetting those things which are behind, . . . I press toward the mark for the prize of the high calling of God in Christ Jesus" (Phil. 3:13).

"This is the day which the Lord hath made. We will rejoice and be glad in" (Ps. 118:24).

If you want to grow and stay positive, you may have to change your mind-set about all of life.

For instance, there is a story of the lepers told in the Old Testament (2 Kings 7:3-8).

The law at that particular time held that a leper was not allowed to enter the city, or else he would die. The lepers were outside the city and were dying of starvation. Finally one suggested to an other, "If we stay here, we know we will surely die, but if we go into the town, maybe they will have mercy on us and we will not die." They argued back and forth. Finally they decided to go in. They discovered the city had been deserted, and the people were literally run off, so there was food and clothing for them all. The moral of the story is: they took the chance and decided they would try. They were awarded with life. Many people die or are living a "dead" life because they don't try.

The story indicates that we may think we are in an impossible situation when what we must learn is to move out and to see what happens. As the leper said: "Surely if we stay here, we will die." And that happens to many, many people because they do not try.

An unknown sage once observed: "A rut is nothing more than a grave with both ends knocked out." And many people in life fit themselves into a rut, and the end result of a rut is the same as a grave.

One time I walked into a used car dealer's office in Helena, Arkansas. He had a sign hanging in his office that read: "When you have stopped changing, you have stopped." Of course, to him that was a motivator for people to continue to change cars periodically. But it is a way of life. Principles never change. Methodology always does, and we need to change with our methods, or soon we will be swallowed up.

For instance, I recently drove to New Mexico by way of Kansas, Nebraska, Colorado, and Texas. Being an avid reader of Louis L'Amour Westerns, I couldn't help thinking, as I was driving across the plains, that a hundred years ago the mode of transportation was covered wagons. There was the fear of the Indians, the fear of wild beasts, the fear of being robbed and murdered, the fear of no law existing "West of the Pecos." The thought of travel a hundred years ago was appalling. No roads, or at best a trail, no signs or road maps.

There I was riding in my motor home at about fifty miles an hour in air-conditioned comfort on a beautiful super highway. Everything along the super highway looked good—new, smooth, and clean. There were also several hundred miles that I took state highways. How the countryside had changed. In a sense I drifted back in many areas at least fifty years as the highways narrowed down, the towns were small and rundown, and the population was poor, evidenced by the housing. Very few modern stores, homes, or businesses existed. To think that 100 or 150 years ago no highways existed—only dirt trails, covered wagons, heat and dust, lack of water, and limited food. My point: What if I were a person who did not want to change with the times and still followed the dirt trails in an old covered wagon behind horses, with the choking heat and dust and strong possibilities of bad food and poor water, if any at all. I would be in a fix. One must be willing to change with the times, adapt to new methods, be open to new ideas, and be willing to try new ways. Improvement can often occur with change.

In church life, too many times there is an attitude of, "We want it like the old days." That's an interesting statement. What are the old days? Does that mean going back to offering up sacrifices like in the Old Testament? Does it mean meeting in a one-room building with oil lamps for light and wood stoves for heat? Does it mean meeting out in the prairie under a tree with a preacher who comes around once a month? What does the "old days" mean?

The question has good intent, but if followed will have deadly results. Basic principles never change, but methods do.

We must keep up with the times, use the methods that are current, and maintain the mind-set of always looking to the future for improvement in presenting the plan of God to more people. If we did not adapt for progress, many people would be lost. For instance, today one of the most superb ways of reaching people is through the media of motion pictures, television, and satellites. It is exciting to realize that through satellite it is possible for an entire world to hear the gospel of Christ! It is also possible through the BTN program of the Baptist Sunday School Board for people in the entire nation to learn more about doing an effective job for God. What does it require to reach people? Change of the right kind. Therefore, be willing to change, to improve, because as one improves, it causes other people to be motivated your own motivational level increases tremendously and helps you to stay positive, which influences others.

Note Pad on the Nightstand

Place a blank note pad on your nightstand—also a pen or pencil. When you wake up in the middle of the night with ideas on your mind, you will be able to scribble enough of a sentence in the dark—or a phrase or words. Possibly wake up totally, turn on the light, and write out the whole idea or ideas, along with solutions to what has been going on in your mind. If you say to yourself, while half asleep, *I will remember what that is, and when I wake up in the morning I will jot it down.* The problem is that too often you can't think of any words, phrases, or ideas to trigger your mind in order to bring from your subconscious mind those thoughts which surface during sleep. But words or phrases written on a pad during the night will help you recall the idea, and you will have the solution to a problem or an idea that will put you closer to your goal.

The mind is a marvelous "computer." It records every fact, incident, feeling, remark, and idea both related and unrelated, and is a historical filing cabinet of your entire life. In your waking hours you have established certain thinking patterns to solving problems, creating ideas, or emotionally handling situations. When sleep comes, relaxation sets in, and the brain is allowed to bypass trained thinking patterns and "compute" freely from the total reserve of facts and feelings, using all the energy to reveal solutions, ideas, and answers untapped when awake.

The note pad by the bed will be a worthy change in your maximizing of time and energy.

Be a List Maker

To reinforce a positive mind-set for yourself and to build faith in yourself, it is good to begin each day by listing what you would like to accomplish. Using this process does several things for you. (1) It gives you direction for the day; (2) it causes you to think of things that would be worth attaining; (3) it establishes priority levels and values about what you give your time to.

God's Three Gifts

Earlier in the book I said, God gives everyone three *things* (1) time, (2) energy, and (3) resources. Resources can be divided into two different categories—one being human resources—that is, someone else helping you to accomplish a task, and the other being money or something equivalent to money, since it does require a certain amount of money to accomplish some goals.

The question each one of us must decide is: "How am I going to use my time most effectively?" In the process of utilizing time, one also spends energy. Some tasks, some goals, some opportunities require big expenditures of energy. When one sees the reward for the energy that has been expended, the cost is possibly too high and is not worth it. So a person must back off and say, "To accomplish that goal was too costly in time and in energy. Either I need to change my goal, or I need to find a more effective and efficient way of accomplishing that goal with less time and less energy."

Here again, not only energy but resources come into play. Sometimes goals will be too costly for the corresponding results, either in personnel or in finances. All of us have an equal amount of time, that is, twenty-four hours a day, and yet there are some people who are paupers and beggars while others are multimillionaires, and both started life equal. When it comes to considering the energy, many of us will vary since our energy levels are different. However, all of us have energy whether we be youths or senior adults. But each of us has varying degrees of energy. How we put that energy to effective operation is not neccesarily dependent on the age of the person, but how well we use the energy. This is true about resources we have at our disposal. How well do we utilize them and maximize those resources?

You need to be a list maker. This will cause a person to decide consciously how he/she is using his/her time, energy, and resources. At the close of the day, one can sit down to evaluate the accomplishments by marking those items on the list as being accomplished. The length and content of the list will vary from time to time, according to the day and the personality of the person. For instance, the list might look like this on a Saturday: Sweep the patio and garage, cut the grass, trim the trees and hedges, pick up branches, rake the grass, leaves, and small twigs, and paint the shutters.

You look at your list and might say to yourself, *There is no way I can accomplish all of this in one day. It is impossible.*

Immediately you have established in your own mind a negative attitude and have mused to yourself, *There is no need of trying to get it all done.* You find yourself starting the day defeated, when it would be just as easy to say: "Is there a way to reduce the energy expended in the amount of time it may take to do each job individually? Is there a way to combine jobs? Here's a possibility."

One must wait for the grass to dry before cutting, so this means that mowing can't start until sometime after 8 or 9 in the morning. Consider painting the shutters on the west side of the house in the shade. This could be done first. Next, the trees could be trimmed and the branches picked up. Then move to the north side of the house and paint the shutters there. This keeps one in the shade all the time, where it is still cool, plus giving you a change of pace. Many jobs become boring and tedious over long periods of time.

Next would come trimming the hedges and bushes. By now it is probably afternoon. You've finished lunch, and you arrive at the east side to paint the shutters. Again the house is in the shade on that side. Now follows the mowing of the grass. Because you are a thinking person, you have a grass bag attachment on the lawnmower which catches the grass, the leaves, and small twigs left over from the hedge, bush, and tree trimming. The grass is mowed, and you sweep the patio and the garage, put away the equipment, and finish painting the south side shutters on the house, now in the cool of the evening.

Because you worked in sequence, you didn't cross yourself. You had variety all day long. You kept yourself in the cool which reduced your energy expenditure and accomplished all the tasks you had set out for the day. Whereas, if you hadn't used the sequential order, you would've stood the chance of sweeping the garage or patio, and then mowing grass and cutting limbs and shrubs, thus causing some of the mess to go on to a freshly swept patio or to be tracked into a garage. You would've ended up on a ladder painting in the hot sun and getting very bored after three or four windows.

The point is: making a list helps put jobs in sequence to maximize time, energy, and resources. This is an element of time management, in other words, getting the most out of every minute and every dollar for the least amount of energy and expenditure of resources. Therefore, become a list maker to multiply your accomplishments in a given day, and maximize your time, energy, and resources.

The same principle is true in your job and your home life. God gives us all the same three gifts: time, energy, and resources (people and money)

If part of your time is used in activities that do not cause growth toward your goal, support reaching your goal, or promote accomplishment of your goal, you have lost time forever, and your priority (your goal) has been robbed.

If you became involved in an activity that did not cause growth toward, support of, or promotion toward the goal, you expended energy. That energy is used up and lost forever, diverted from the priority—your goal.

If you became involved in an activity and money was spent that did not cause growth, support, or promotion toward the desired end, resources were diverted from the priority.

What do you want to see happen?

Take a blank sheet of paper, and for sixty seconds think words, things, or activities you want out of life. Write whatever comes to your mind without analyzing them.

After you have done this, analyze the words you have written. Some of the words are useless, so drop them from the list. Write a sentence or paragraph about each word or phrase. Decide which is number 1, 2, 3, etc. This will help you to establish a true priority with meaning. Once the priorities have been decided on, goals can be established with validity.

Setting Smart Goals

Proverbs 29:18: "Where there is no vision, the people perish."

The apostle Paul wrote, "I press toward the mark" (Phil. 3:14).

Both the Old and New Testaments talk of having goals and working toward them.

If the leadership of a church does not know where it wants to go, how can a congregation?

Enough "preaching"—on with the goal-setting.

For a "going, growing" church, goals should be set in the area of:

- Enrollment
- Attendance
- Training awards
- New units
- Workers' meeting attendance
- Baptisms
- Worship service attendance

• Contacts

In some churches the above list will be longer. In other churches it may be modified.

When one makes a goal, it should be a *smart* goal. Using an acrostic, let's see the characteristics of a smart goal:

S—Specific
M—Measurable
A—Attainable
R—Rewarding
T—Tangible/Time frame

Specific

The goal should be specific and easy to identify. For example, assume you want to increase the enrollment by 100. It is not *about* 100 or *near* 100, or *hope* for 100—*it is 100.* Another specific in goal-setting would be to ask each department of the Sunday School for a specific number. For example, you would say to the adult director, "Can you increase your enrollment twenty-five people in the next year?" The department director would ask each teacher for a specific enrollment goal number. "Teacher, can you increase your enrollment by five next year?"

As you can see, these are specific goals for each part of the organization of the Sunday School. When a person understands *his* responsibility, he tends more toward reaching the goal. Therefore, make the goals specific.

Measurable

When making the decision on goals, those goals must be measurable. Listing specific numbers makes them measurable. To make a goal measurable it must have a time frame. For example, when a department director is talking to the Adult teacher and says, "Your enrollment goal is eight for the year. Do you think you can enroll two people each quarter? By dividing the goal in smaller increments, the reality of attainment is keener.

All goals should be measurable. Otherwise, how will you know when you have accomplished the goal? How will you gauge how close you are to accomplishing the goal? How will you realize when you are already over halfway to the goal? Make sure your goals have measuring devices. You recognize the goal is specific and measurable because of the use of numbers, time frame, and the like.

Attainable

A goal should be attainable. This fact in itself will help you to reach that goal. To make a goal attainable, facts must be given to support the possibility of reaching it. For example, if an adult department were given a goal of increasing its enrollment by twenty-five, it should have a more than adequate list of prospects.

Given a number of approaches to reach the prospects, the department should have sufficient space to absorb the increase, ample furniture to seat the people, enough leadership to teach, and adequate assistance from the church office to attain the goal. It is better to make a goal small and attainable. Then, larger goals can be set for later attainment. Whenever one goal is accomplished, set a new one.

By the time I had reached fifty years of age, I had set a goal of having ten rental properties in ten years, for the purpose of having additional income at retirement. To accomplish that goal I began to read a number of books, periodicals, and newspapers, and listened to speakers on the subject of real estate and how to be a success.

One book I read was, *How I Took a Thousand Dollars and Became a Millionnaire.* In this book the statement was made, in essence, "A time will come when you will be able to buy a house and never take a dollar out of your pocket." I thought that was a bunch of bologna, but I did it, the reason being I had filled my mind with considerable information. If you "bone up" on a subject, when the time comes to make a decision, you will have a vast reservoir to draw from, and more than likely will make the right decision. Therefore—study, absorb, and observe. Sensitize your total being to becoming alert in subject areas of interest to you. When the time is right you will instinctively make the correct decisions. My ten-year goal was reached in three and one-half years.

Rewarding

When goals are specific, measurable, attainable, and reached, they are very rewarding. It is joyful to make an accomplishment, to reach a plateau. The emotional self feels good; the spiritual self deep inside hears the verse, "Well done, thou good and faithful servant" (Matt. 25:-21).

There is happiness in sharing with others, the team effort of meeting the challenge and winning. True joy cannot be measured in dollars, but is, in itself, a full reward.

A smart goal should be *rewarding.* There is satisfaction in knowing that you have attained. Sometimes there are physical, monetary, emotional, educational, and other things that constitute a rewarding goal. To some, the fact of accomplishing the goal is reward enough.

Here are ten areas that motivate people to action:

1. Fear	5. Wealth
2. Prestige	6. Recognition
3. Security	7. Acceptability
4. Health	8. Praise

9. Self-Aggrandizement   10. Intimidation

Most people directly or indirectly ask themselves anytime a challenge is directed toward them, "What am I going to get out of this?"

Therefore, all smart goals should be rewarding so a person can feel, "I have accomplished," "I have received," for however any of the preceding ten areas might have motivated them.

Tangible/Time Frame

A smart goal is *tangible.* A tangible goal must be related to the overall purpose of what is being attempted, tangible in the sense that minor goals are established to attain a larger goal. All minor goals relate directly to the accomplishment of the larger goal.

For example, when going through the seminary, I had a goal of graduating with a degree. Taking daily quizzes in a class and passing them led to passing for the half-semester time, which led to passing for the semester, which led to passing the course for the year, which led to passing all the courses for the year, which led to going into the next year of study and passing all of those exams. Each of those quizzes was tangible in relation to the overall goal of graduation. So, set small, short-term, tangible goals to help you accomplish your major goal.

Every goal should have a time frame. *By a certain date* the goal should be reached. Then new goals and time frames should be set for accomplishment.

A time frame in which the goal can be evaluated and measured in progress is necessary.

The goal should be over a period of time, say one year, five years, ten years, or possibly in short increments of one month, three months, six months, nine months, or twelve months.

Time frames in small increments with numerical measurement will gauge the progress being made.

Example 1: In ten years my goal was to reach a certain monetary goal. I discovered I could attain my goal by acquiring rental property. For me to stay on target toward my goal, I had to establish a time frame for reaching the goal—ten years. Each year, if I were to reach the monetary goal, I had to attain a certain number of dollars' worth of rental property. I divided the year into quarters. Doing this I acquired so many dollars' worth of assets per quarter.

Example 2. I needed to lose thirty pounds to be in better health and in good physical condition. I set the goal for me to lose that weight in six months. I divided the time to lose five pounds each month. I visualized it on the calendar. Each week the goal was to lose a pound or more. I set a specific day each week to weigh. Each Sunday morning before going to church I wrote my weight on the calendar. By establishing a specific time, a specific day, and a specific amount to lose, I set my mind to prepare for the week. I became a winner each week. For now my goal was specific and measurable, showing attainable goals. I weighed 246 pounds on March 1, 1984, and by the end of August I weighed 216 pounds. You can do what you want to do if you want to do it badly enough!

Remember that smart goals must be specific, measurable, attainable, rewarding, and tangible—with a time frame.

To attain my weight loss goals and be a winner each week, I changed and established certain eating habits. I quit snacking between meals, I totally cut out sweets and reduced the amount of starches. I even fasted one day a week over a period of several weeks. I carried a 3 x 5 card in my pocket on which I could write down everything I ate and drank during the course of a day. I wrote down the approximate number of calories each morsel was worth. After a month I could see what results were accomplished. I then adjusted myself and prescribed a program accordingly to reach my desired goal.

A good suggestion is to buy clothes which will fit you only when you reach your desired weight. Place them where they are visible each day as a reminder of another reward you will receive when the goal is accomplished.

You can do whatever you set your mind to do. The clothes idea is not too far out of line. Create some symbol of the reward you will receive when you reach the desired goal. It becomes a constant motivator.

Biblical Backing for Goals

A number of places in the Scriptures you will find references to goals:

1. "Set your affections on things above (Col. 3:2).

2. "I press toward the mark" (Phil. 3:14).

3. "Run the race" (1 Cor. 9:24).

4. "I can do all things through Christ" (Phil. 4:13).

5. "Mountain, be thou removed" (Mark 11:23).

6. "Thy word have I hid in my heart" (Ps. 119:11).

7. "Where there is no vision, the people perish" (Prov. 29:18).

(Now add three or more of your verses.)

8.

9.

10.

As you "search the Scriptures" you will find many more.

Spiritual Goals

Scripture memory: One verse a week, fifty-two a year. How many did you learn last year? Look what you could do during the next fifty-two weeks. Use a 3 x 5 card and write a Scripture verse you wish to memorize. Place it on the mirror in the bathroom, over the kitchen sink, or in some other place where you spend short periods of time doing something else. Learn to maximize your time. You *can do* two or more things at once. As you shave or put on your makeup, you can glance at the card and quote the verse. As you wash dishes, fold the towels and linens, or pour a glass of water, you can quote a verse. If you ride a bus or carpool it to work, you can carry the card, glance at it, and quote it.

Bible reading: It is possible to read the Bible through daily in the course of a year if the person sets the pace of three chapters a day and five on Sunday. Beginning on January 1 one will complete reading the entire Bible by December 27. You can start the first of any month. You do not have to wait until January 1. In fact, the Scriptures declares, "Now is the accepted time" (2 Cor. 6:2). It is possible to read the New Testament in less than three months with this approach.

James wrote: "To him that knoweth to do good and doeth it not, to him it is sin" (4:17).

I mentioned earlier that negative thinking is a learned process. However, through changed learning and training, your thinking can be made positive. Don't give up.

Develop a willingness to persevere. Stick with it. Be dissatisfied with incompletion and mediocrity. This is the determination that produces a winner, a successful, positive, creative person. You can be that person. Say out loud to yourself, "I can do." Say it again, "I can do!"

Look at each experience as a learning experience. Write what you learned, even if you failed for the moment. If you learned something, even if you profited from your mistakes, there is a degree of success and a step closer to total success. Analyze what you have done. Visualize what needs to be changed to make it work and try it again. When you keep trying you are closer to success.

To make something better, select something that is good, change it to meet your needs and to fit you, your personality, where you are, as you are, with what you have and are. Then, it becomes the best because it is yours with your own personality and needs built in. In this book are many ideas, many of which may need to be changed slightly to fit you. Now you have the best there is and it is yours—no longer mine.

Buying Boats with Holes and Making Money

Learn to see things not as they are, but as they could be. For example: I have bought boats with holes in them and made money.

Many people look at boats with holes in the bottom as useless objects. Let me give you several suggestions on how to look at something not as it is, but as it could be. Here is a boat with a hole in it. What can you do with a boat that has a hole in it?

1. The boat possibly could be repaired and used again. I've done that.
2. You could cut the boat up if it is wood and use it for firewood. I've done that.
3. You could use it as playground equipment, since children have a wonderful imagination. To them it becomes one of the greatest playground pieces of equipment available. I've done that.

4. It could be used as landscape. If you have seafood restaurants in your area, you are aware of the old, rotten shells of boats as part of their layout. I've sold a number of those.

5. You can put four bales of hay in a boat, tow it out to about sixteen feet of water, and sink it. Come back in several weeks, and you'll have the best fishing hole you've ever found.

6. Some boats are large enough to be dry-docked and used as a retreat or cabin hideaway near the shore. It beats building a whole cabin.

Therefore, when you see something that looks useless, ask the question in your own mind, *What else could it be?* Let your imagination run free. It will amaze you "what it can be."

As Christians, remember how we were when Christ found us. He took us when we were useless and nothing, and began building us into something that is a prized possession.

Train yourself to use your imagination to "color outside the lines." Think, but don't be locked in by tradition, habit, or necessarily what others think.

Learn to *see* with your *ears,* to *hear* with your *eyes,* to *taste* with your *nose!* You say quickly, "This' impossible." But blind people see with their ears all the time; the deaf hear with their eyes. It is not impossible to take one of your senses and train it to respond in a different manner. When you smell the fragrance of charcoal steaks, your salivary glands immediately begin to flow, and you can taste how delicious a steak might be.

Motivation is a self-learned technique. *If you cannot motivate yourself, you cannot motivate others.* Motivation can be like breathing. A child is born with self-motivation, an instinctive element of survival. A parent knowingly or unknowingly subdues motivation in a child—or enhances it. Therefore, begin saying to yourself, "I can do more than I'm doing. I can change. I am somebody. I can think, I can be, I am of worth. I am important. I am of value. I am a person. I am needed. I can do what I want to do. If I want to do it badly enough, I will."

Visualize the Goal

What you visualize in your mind, can be.

Success doesn't come the way you think—success comes *because* of the way you think. That is my firm conviction.

You are becoming what you think. The question is, What do you think about? Do you even spend time simply thinking? For instance, as you start each day, do you think, What would I like to accomplish? Do you make a list? Do you think through that list? Are some of the items on that list really worth being listed or attempted? Do you think about how much time that item (or items) will take? Do you think of how to accomplish what you are thinking? Do you write a strategy of any kind? Do you make tentative plans? The Scripture states "For as he thinketh in his heart, so is he" (Prov. 23:7). What do you think about? Cultivate time to yourself just to think, plan, set some goals, and create some images that can be seen daily or periodically as a reminder.

Signs for Attitude Change

Surround yourself with positive sayings. For example: "The Secret to Success Is Involvement. The more people you have involved, the more successful you will become in the project you are attempting."

"When you stop changing, you stop."

"A winner never quits, and a quitter never wins."

If you are a teacher of a Sunday School class, as I am, a sign that would prove effective in an adult classroom or department would be: "The proof of good teaching is not necessarily the size of your class, but the proof of good teaching is how many times you have multiplied yourself." A teacher must realize that he has a saturation point as to the number of lives he can affect. Psychology tells us that we influence ten people positively and/or negatively, but each of us has a circle of at least ten we influence. When you put this into a classroom setting, you quickly see how limited one might become in teaching.

But if you lead someone from your class to teach elsewhere, you have, in a sense, multiplied your teaching by ten. Therefore, ask yourself how many people have been led into teaching or training from your youth or adult class. This gives a fair idea of how many times you have multiplied yourself. Last year twelve people went out from my class. That means I multiplied myself twelve times. Interestingly, if a person has sat under your teaching for a period of time, even one or two years, they knowingly and unknowingly have picked up a number of your mannerisms, characteristics, enthusiasm, style, methodology, and involvement in their teaching. The reason is you are *the* example they have seen in teaching. For instance, if you use a chalkboard to illustrate in your teaching or group involvement, or questions and answers, or a lecture method, or looking up of Scripture verses, they will also pick up those same processes and techniques.

Create Mental Pictures

An exercise I often use in conferences is to ask the participants to take a blank sheet of paper and for sixty seconds write words, phrases, or sentences that race across their minds when thinking about goals. Such as, What would I like to see happen to my Sunday School in the next twelve months? What are my goals? What do I want for me? and the like. Then, as quickly as they can, they are asked to write down any phrases, ideas, or words allowing their imaginations to run free. The surprising fact is, in a short time their minds seem to stop thinking. After about fifteen to twenty seconds they stop and, with a blank stare on their faces, they sit waiting for the next thirty-forty seconds to go by. Their minds go blank since they haven't spent much time thinking about goals. After they have written a number of words and phrases, I ask them to look at them and write a sentence or paragraph about each word or phrase.

Expand the idea on that word just to discover what depth or possibilities might come from it. The second phase is basically to imagine "what if." They now move from running-free imagination to imagine, "What if we did this or that?" This can be done only by thinking and expanding on the words or phrases. This second step is actually an analysis of what they have written. It will help them to know if there are some possibilities in what they have written. Eliminate those words that, from all appearances, have absolutely no meaning or possibility. The third step is to look at what has been written in the expanded form—then to decide what is the number-one priority and possibility. Then two, three, four, and five. I encourage them to prioritize what they have written.

Going through this exercise, one discovers he can make

his Sunday School grow, and can make things change and happen in his life. They can lead people to change and set goals, working toward those goals.

An example: A class might decide to set a goal of increasing the Sunday School enrollment. Let's assume the class has fifteen on the roll. They decide among themselves to increase the enrollment by twelve for the coming year. Remember that the secret to success is involvement. The more people you have involved in attempting a goal, the more successful your goal will be. Discussion takes place as to what would be a meaningful, challenging goal for the class. When a person has input into a goal, at that moment he/she has made a commitment to help reach that goal.

Therefore, lead the class to make a wise goal. Twelve is a specific number. It is easy to understand. It is easy to identify. The goal is measurable. Identifying the number twelve made it measurable. Deciding on one new member a month poses the time frame for the goal. This makes it possible for the class to see whether it is ahead or behind each month. There is the need for ample prospects to reach the goal of twelve new members.

Remember that each person has at least ten circles of influence, so the class has immediately at their fingertips at least 150 people they come in contact with each week and influence. It is understood all 150 would not be prospects. However, surely every member would become aware of at least one prospect—now to solving the problem of having enough prospects and making the goal attainable. Probe each person's mind, asking the question, "Who do you know that does not *attend* Sunday School?" To help probe the mind, the questions may be asked, "Is it a neighbor across the street, to the right, to the left, behind you?" Are some of your friends not in Sunday School?" Or if the class is a group of students, "Who do you go to school with that does not attend?" "What about a relative who lives in the church community but does not attend?" There are a number of questions that could be asked, questions which would cause the mind to think of people and discover prospects they already know and associate with. It is evident, if the Sunday School class accepts you as a member, they will accept your prospect. People have a tendency to think of prospects of like kind.

Now that you have ample prospects, your goal for attaining the increase is possible. You have also stimulated their minds to be aware of other prospects you will contact in the future.

Using Signs for Growth

There are many ways to keep the prospects ever-present in the minds of the class members. Part of the attainment would be to make a small poster and place it in the class to indicate that the goal for the year is *twelve,* and that our quota for this month is *one* new member. A 3 x 5 card could be taped to the back of a chair with the words "New Member" printed on it, which would be a constant visual reminder, silently saying, "Think of reaching a new member." "Who is a prospect I need to invite?" It will also reduce the process of when a potential new member does come into the class. Instead of handing a visitor slip, an enrollment card would be handed to that person with the statement made, "Please fill out this enrollment card. We want you as a new member." This approach is working on the goal and keeping a constant awareness to reach people. The goal becomes rewarding when a new member fills out an enrollment card and joins the class.

Soon after joining the class, a new member should be asked if he/she knows any prospects for the class. A new convert especially knows more lost people than a person who has been a Christian for a long time. The reason is that many of their friends are unbelievers. This gives the new member or convert an immediate opportunity of service and feeling a part of the class—wanted and being needed.

The element of reward multiplies itself many times over when a goal is set and accomplished. The tangible part is attaining the small, short-term, monthly goals which all lead toward the ultimate goal of having an increase in enrollment of twelve by the end of the year.

There are examples of creating an image or signs to lead and motivate people into involvement in a Sunday School class.

Let's think in another area of our life, of creating an image or a symbol to reach a desired goal. Most people have personal goals and desires for their own lives. Some want to be the supervisor, the head of a department, or the president of the company. These goals are all good. One must ask oneself, What might it take to fill that responsibility?

Again, use the example or exercise that was earlier illustrated of allowing the imagination to run free and to imagine "what if," thus creating images in your mind. Once the image is created, take a pad of paper and list a number of questions, such as, How does the person you have created in your mind dress, speak, express himself, that indicate he is a supervisor or leader? How does he walk? What manners does he manifest? What kind of a car does he drive? The list will be extended, the more you study the person. That person is holding a position because of certain characteristics possessed, such as, even-tempered, a listener, an observer, a student of human nature, and so on. Once you have identified these characteristics, ask yourself, "What in my life do I need to change? What positive characteristics do I possess that need to be magnified and strengthened? What physical things might I do to begin looking like the person for the position? What habits do I need to establish or break? It would be good to condense the identification of the character or image onto a 3 x 5 card, or possibly several cards. Place one on the bathroom mirror where you prepare ready for the day. Run those ideas through your mind so they will be a part of you throughout the day. Carry them on card in your pocketbook or jacket—on your person at all times. Remember you are becoming what you think.

In the Old Testament, incidentally, there was a practice similar to this for the Jew who wanted to keep the law. He wore what was called a frontlet on his forehead or on his arm. The frontlet was a small box which contained Hebrew Scripture texts which made him consciously aware of the law of God ever-present around him. In a sense, by carrying a card, you are following the same concept. A glance at the card reestablishes or calls to mind the desired goal, and keeps you on track toward the ultimate goal.

In your office or workplace, a card could be placed inside your desk drawer or locker, so every time you open it, a mere glance at the card will make you aware. Or it could be a symbol in your work area. Every time you glanced at it it would recall your desired goals.

Create a Symbol of the Goal

Allow me a personal illustration. In 1980 I had a desired financial goal as mentioned earlier in the book. It had been on my mind for several months. I was attempting to figure out how it could be attained. One day while driving between Waco and Dallas, Texas, a plan jelled in my mind about how to accomplish the goal. I was driving a rental car. I pulled off the road and looked for some paper to write down what had gone through my mind. A rental car matchbook was lying on the floor. I picked it up, wrote down the location, the date, the goal how it could be attained, and the completion date. That matchbook cover from that 1980 date until now is on my dresser. Everytime I go to that dresser I glance at the matchbook and am reminded of my goal.

As of this writing, the goal and process are still on target. In all probability, I will hit the goal, but let's assume I don't. There is always the possibility of falling short or going over the goal. Whichever happens, it certainly will be far beyond where I was in 1980.

It was a smart goal because it had specific, measurable, attainable, rewarding, and tangible increments to it. Therefore, plan smart goals and create a symbol like the matchbook—simple as it may seem, that will be visible to you on a daily or periodical basis. It keeps the vision, the mind-set, the direction, the anticipation ever before you and enhances the joy and satisfaction when attained.

Establish Positive Reading Habits

Read material that will build your mind-set into positive thinking. Read books about people who have overcome tremendous odds. Read books about people that made their millions. Read books in the areas you are interested in or in which you have goals set. You soon will discover overcoming, successful people are no different from you. In fact, in many instances you have more going for you than they did. They overcame the odds, and so can you.

Establish the practice of associating with positive, energetic, enthusiastic people who are winners and successful. When someone in a group begins to degrade or negate someone, say to yourself, *Now that person being talked about, what are his/her qualities? What can they do that is good?* Speak out a positive word for that person. Determine there is some good in everyone. The difficulty that happens if you do not follow this practice is that you will consciously or subconsciously find yourself identifying with the negative, and it will pull you down.

Remember, you can always walk away from the group. Avoid negative thoughts negative conversation, and negative company. A popular song a few years back was "Look for the Silver Lining." Another good song went, "accentuate the positive." So do that.

Love Motivates

When a person is in love, the impossible becomes possible. The person in love really discovers he/she can do what he wants to do if he wants to do it badly enough. There seems to be no end to energy. The person becomes tireless in effort. Strength never seems to wane; waking hours are filled with joy; no dark clouds prevail long in his life. If shades of night appear on his horizon there is the positive awareness a dawn is sure to come, so darkness will be only momentary.

I know a woman whose nature is reserved, quiet, nonaggressive, subdued, tranquil, peaceful, who rarely raised her voice in excitement. Then she became a "band parent." Her child joined the high school marching band. Two-hundred youth perform in this band. The freshman year was a time for this new band mother to become involved, learning, and feeling a part of the whole.

The sophomore year was a time for her to grow actively in the group. Her personality began to change. Time for service became intensified.

The junior year was compounded with continual excitement—places to go, trips to sponsor, funds to be raised, band competitions to attend, and a myriad of hours, energy, and money expended. Never a moment of reservation or question "Is this important?" Of course, it was important.

The senior year yielded its greatest excitement as her son became president of the high school band. That year intense involvement was at its peak. More hours and energy were expended. The idea of missing an event was never considered. Total support of all concerts, contests, field practices, and football games was deemed absolutely necessary.

That quiet, reserved, nonaggressive woman, during the four years of band, became a screaming banshee during band contests, uninhibited at football games, had endless enthusiasm in fund-raising, and gave freely financially to band causes.

Why did all of this happen? It was, and is, a deep-seated love for her child, his welfare, his joy, his success, and his acceptance as a leader.

Her rewards were both tangible and intangible: seeing the band winning the coveted Champion of Champions Trophy, the Governor's Trophy, her son as the "chosen one" of the entire band as president, the self-confidence given to her son for life, and his positive attitudes of assurance to succeed when challenges arise.

Was it worth it all? Her love declared it was. True love is the highest degree of motivation.

Therefore, fall in love, afresh, anew, again.
Fall in love with your job.
Fall in love with your family.
Fall in love with your husband/wife.
Fall in love with an activity.
Fall in love with your church.
Fall in love with your denomination.

Fall in love with Christ—the greatest, highest love of all, and all the above will become easier, with greater personal rewards than ever before.

Knowledge Motivates

The more knowledge you possess about an area of life, a job, or an activity, the greater the excitement. The desire to learn more about what "turns you on" becomes intensified.

Become more aggressive about gaining information of your interests. Increasing knowledge sharpens your skills, your sensitivity, your awareness.

Knowledge becomes the key to making good judgments. Knowledge ushers in success, satisfaction, recognition, rewards, confidence, and credibility.

Knowledge is never wasted. Every experience through reading, activity, and involvement is stored into the computer of the mind ready to be called upon instantaneously when the need arises.

Build your reservoir with positive information, factual bits and pieces to be assimilated into right results when issues develop.

Many times I have had to fill out reports after leading a conference or event. There has been one question on the report that has always caused me to laugh. The question was, "How much time did you spend preparing for this event?" Now I know they wanted an answer in hours. But being the individual thinker (or is it "stinker"?) I am, I would write "all my life." Fortunately, that question is no longer on the reports I fill out.

In reality, that answer was more accurate than putting down the number of hours. For when you lead, you do spend hours in preparation, but as you deliver what you have prepared, there is always the unexpected question, the attitude of a group, the events that transpired before the presentation, the assumption you had about your audience before the meeting perhaps being incorrect. You are then forced to "think on your feet," and automatically you have no choice but to draw upon knowledge that was gained long before the preparation for the meeting took place. It may come from knowledge and experience that was gained ten, twenty, or thirty years ago—or even back to childhood days.

Now you can understand why I answer—"All my life." Spontaneity adds freshness to a presentation. Leaving your notes, outline, or material, and dipping into your vast reservoir of related information adds zest, life, and excitement to your "canned" speech.

Therefore, add as much knowledge as you can through every possible method of gathering information. It never will be lost; it will be used some day when you least expect it and need it most.

Money Motivates

Some religious people have problems with this concept, having the idea that it is sinful to have money or to think about money to motivate them into action.

My feeling is they are not being totally honest with themselves. Let me illustrate. The person who thinks money does not motivate him/her would find great disappointment if:

- He did not receive an increase in salary when performance review comes around
- He did not advance to a better job when the opportunity came
- He were asked to take a cut in salary
- Suddenly he was without a job

All people have various desires for themselves and their families. They want the acceptable

- home
- job
- auto
- clothes
- education
- security
- travel
- family needs
- charitable gifts
- prestigious items (second car, boat, cycle, swimming pool, jewelry, paintings, vacation home, furs, stocks, and bonds)

If these desires are recognizable in your life, you have to admit everyone of these desires take money. Therefore, money is a part of your motivation. Let's look at the Scriptures for the answer to the question, "Is it sinful to have or make money?" "The *love* of money is the root of all evil" (1 Tim. 6:10). Money is not the root of all evil—inordinate love for it is.

The sin comes not in having money or acquiring it but in letting the acquisition of money become an obsession with you. Some love money to the extent they do not share it with others. Some withhold its use that would benefit the family. Sometimes the love of money becomes so strong that people even withhold the benefits it could afford them. The example of the character Scrooge in Dickens's *Christmas Carol* shows how Scrooge with all his wealth deprived himself of many personal benefits he could have had *using* his wealth.

Therefore, accept the need for money, and go after it. Accomplish those desires that benefit your family, yourself, and others.

Early in my ministry I was one who had the mistaken concept that if one had the desire to make money, it was sinful. There were times I actually promoted that view.

Deep in my being there was the constant struggle of wanting to make money. Finally I allowed the desire to surface my conscious mind. One day I verbalized the thoughts. "I want to make money." How strange that sounded to my ears, "I want to make money." Is it true? Is it right? Is it sinful?

My supervisor, who has the gift of analyzing a situation, helped me the most with this dilemma. His analysis was, "Neil, it's not money that motivates you, but what it represents to you. For you it is a measuring device on the ladder of success."

The moment the statement was made, my feelings of remorse, guilt, and anguish were removed. Then he added another statement, "God controls and blesses. If one can keep in mind that these blessings come from God and share these blessings in whatever way God leads, there is no reason to have guilt."

If you have feelings like I've expressed, verbalize them. Ask God for direction, and if He blesses in this area, keep listening to Him about how to use it. Money does motivate.

What Else Motivates?

A number of things motivate people. Look at the following list. Ask yourself, What motivates me? You will identify with several of these words. Give thought to those high identifiable areas. You may already have identified with those listed. Study the ones following and discover which stand out in your mind.

Those identifiable areas can be stepping stones to your success; they can be your strength. Begin to think of ways to maximize your time, energy, and resources in those areas.

Here are some areas to consider. The right kind of *pride* motivates, and so does *recognition, prestige, acceptance, praise, success, beauty, music,* and various *goals.* Sometimes we are motivated by emotions that are poor reasons for being motivated, such as *guilt* and *fear.* Other unworthy motivators you will become aware of can be changed into a positive mind-set.

Let us move from the lower reasons of motivation to the highest.

The Love of Christ Motivates

Paul wrote: "For the love of Christ constraineth us." (2 Cor. 5:14). What does the word *constrain* mean? A number of meanings give credence to the concept. "Compels" is one. It is the controlling, driving love of Christ and what He has done for us that *compels* the Christian—not only compels but *forces* us. The understanding, compassionate love of Christ *forces* us as we "grow in the grace, and in the knowledge of . . . Christ" (2 Pet. 3:18). The *force* becomes a *driving force* to accomplish the high calling He has given His followers.

I am reminded of a girl I grew up with. She had tremendous influence on me to attend a religious university where she had recently become a professor. After she taught several years, God called her to China as a missionary teacher. That was thirty-five years ago. She had the love of Christ to give up the prestige of teaching in a university, leave family, home, friends, and the affluent life in America.

The love of Christ drove her to conquer the Chinese language, customs, and another way of life. The love of Christ caused her to live the single life, make new friends, and overcome the months and years of loneliness that no doubt existed.

The love of Christ causes denominational people to "live on the road" 100 to 200 days a year in all types of weather, motel conditions, and food. They give up much family life for one-half to two-thirds of the year. It is difficult for them and all members of the family, and loneliness exists for all members of the family. The love of Christ drives (compels, pushes, moves) them to do these things.

The love of Christ draws followers into foreign missions in times like these when many foreign governments are unstable. In many countries merely being a Westerner is dangerous for one's life. The problem is especially compounded when Christianity is presented in a country with an "official religion." Many missionaries who are doctors, nurses, and teachers could easily have a better life in America, but the love of Christ propels these people to the foreign fields.

It is the love of Christ in church staff people who hear the call to local church work, the long hours given, the seven-day-a-week, twenty-four-hour-a-day availability for many church leaders.

Almost without exception, they do it because of their love of Christ.

This love of Christ, to the person dedicated to His work for their lives, is truly the highest and holiest motivation if the individuals have right relationships with the Almighty God. They will be more adept in discovering and using the motivation most best suited to them.

The love of Christ causes Christians in local churches to give freely of their time, energy, and resources in places of responsibility.

The love of Christ is the highest motivation. Give Christ that priority, and all other considerations will miraculously fall into their proper places.

PART II.
How to Motivate Others

In order to motivate others you yourself must be motivated with working toward your goals in life. Most people have no specific goals. Those people merely exist.

Give people a vision. Read Proverbs 29:18 again.

Many people have little or no vision. They live from day to day in sheer existence. Help them to create a vision, ushering life and joy into their lives. Become enthusiastic, energetic, and creative. The apostle Paul wrote, "Whatsoever state [or situation] I am, therewith to be content" (Phil. 4:11). He was in prison at the time!

Help each person see where his/her part or contribution of time, energy, and resources help accomplish the goal.

Many organizations have multimillion-dollar goals. An example is the Jerry Lewis Muscular Dystrophy Fund. No one person or corporation can give the amount of money needed. So what does Jerry do? He and his board set the goal and divide it into smaller goals, identifiable, tangible goals, which people can see, feel, or identify with.

An example: If you give so many dollars, you will be able to buy a pair of crutches or a wheelchair for an MD child. The dollar goal is broken into specific goals of actual items and services being performed by financial gifts. It is not too exciting or meaningful to say to oneself, *I gave $500 to the Muscular Dystrophy Fund.* It is more satisfying and rewarding to say, *I bought a wheelchair for a child to* *have relief from being bedridden or confined to a room. Now the child can move into the halls with others and out into the sunlight and fresh air.* This gives the donor a warm feeling of satisfaction through his gift. This is what I mean by identifiable, rewarding, tangible goals.

The same is true in many religious mission offerings. Many denominations have million-dollar goals for various emphases. But to the person giving the money it means little or doesn't motivate much when kept on a dollar level.

If the offering dollars were translated into actions, the motivation would accelerate tremendously. For example, mission offerings communicated into actions performed, such as fifty dollars feeds a child for a year, twenty-five dollars educates a person for a year, five-hundred dollars builds a room for a mission school or hospital, communicate desired results and will motivate the giving. It will motivate the gift many times over to be greater than originally thought.

Seeing the dollars translated into actual deeds and actions of lives and buildings motivates people where their heartstrings and feelings can be touched. And they say to themselves, *There stand I only by the grace of God. I would gladly give so others might live.*

See Possibilities in Other People

Learn to look for and see possibilities, potentialities in all people. In children: The Scriptures say, "Train up a child in the way he should go and when he is old, he will not depart from it" (Prov. 22:6). Begin now to involve children in more definite, positive activities of the church in growth, outreach, and contacts.

In youth: Give youth a vision of what they can become. Help them to dream dreams and show them how they can accomplish those dreams for the Lord and for their own future. Give them positive attitudes, goals that can be set and accomplished. Give them affirmation of themselves, their worth, their potential.

In adults: Lead adults to see themselves as individuals with worth, value, and abilities. Everyone can do something. Each person is needed, wanted, and can find a place of service in God's kingdom.

We are all saved to serve, not sit. Christ did not hang on a tree for us to sit, nor did He take the thorns on His brow for us to sit; nor the spear in His side, nor the nails in His feet and hands for us to sit. We need to stop and ask, "Lord, what wouldst thou have me to do?" and then stand and listen for the Lord to speak to us and impress us in an area of opportunities.

We as leaders need to learn to help people find places where they can serve in a church. Remember the secret to success is involvement. The more people involved in a church program the more successful it will be.

"We are saved to serve, not sit."

Where would God have us to serve today?

1. Teachers/workers
2. Outreach leaders/group leaders
3. Bus ministry/drivers/captains/mechanics
4. Volunteer secretaries/weekdays office/one morning/one week/special mailouts
5. Telephoners/census takers
6. Carpenters
7. Volunteer maintenance people/light bulbs/switches outlets/window washers
8. Landscapers/grass/snow/flower   beds/general appearance and maintenance
9. Pickup trucks to haul junk away

10. Poster makers
11. Census takers/junior high/senior high/senior adults
12. Prospecting by using the newspapers
13. Prospect file secretaries by age group
14. Short-term service committees, special decorations/food preparation/special occasions

Use the following space to jot places of service needed.

Five Areas of Life that Need Goals

Administering a growing church requires good leadership, and good leaders are effective because they remain sharp mentally, educationally, physically, financially, and spiritually. Using the five areas of life will motivate other people.

There are five areas of life in which a well-balanced Christian should set goals for effective leadership:

- Religion and spiritual things
- Family and home
- Business and finances
- Education and learning
- Physical condition and health

You and I think in most, if not all, of the above areas. When thinking and setting goals concerning any of these aspects, keep in mind the Scripture, "As he thinketh . . . so is he" (Prov. 23:7).

Sometimes we get discouraged and down on ourselves, thinking, *What's the use? Nobody cares,* etc. When this happens, ask yourself, *Could I be missing the mark in some area of my life?"*

Physical and Health

Ask yourself, *How do I really feel physically?* Be honest with yourself. Do you have any of the following symptoms?

- tired
- not sleeping well
- stopped-up head
- Cold
- achy all over
- run down
- exhausted

The list could go on and on. Some ailments can be corrected in a relatively short time. Go to bed early, even though it may require discipline. Hang a "Do Not Disturb" sign on the door. If necessary, check into a motel for several days—this certainly beats the price of a hospital room. In fact, find out what the daily rate is at the local hospital. Cut the price in half and let that be your *per diem* (money per day to spend) allowance.

Many times discouragement is caused by nothing more than fatigue. Sometimes fatigue also leads us to become critical, short-tempered, and irritable with such pains as headache, backache, neck ache, and even tired feet.

The Scripture tells us to "come ye apart and rest awhile" (Mark 6:31). I have to chuckle to myself when I think of this verse. Dear friend, if you don't come apart, and rest, you may come apart physically.

Rest can take many forms. For some it is the obvious—to catch up on sleep. But for others it may be a diversion. Some find it in hobbies, such as sports, building, fishing, and hunting.

I find a great deal of relaxation in riding my motorcycle, a Honda Gold Wing 1100. It gives me a thrill of power and speed. The constant concentration on what you are doing causes you to forget problems, difficulties, and frustrations —at least while you ride.

Let me give you an idea of the concentration that is necessary to ride a motorcycle. If you turn your head to the right to look at something the bike will drift to the right. The reason is that balance is critical in riding the motorcycle. The shifting of your head shifts your weight and your balance to the right. Consequently, the bike goes to the right.

It doesn't take long to learn that you must keep looking forward. In riding a motorcycle, you don't spend a lot of time "gawking" around.

Also, you must keep in mind that when you are riding sixty miles an hour, for every second, eighty-eight feet of concrete speeds by your feet only six inches away. One wrong move and you go sliding on the concrete—a long, long distance.

So you learn to concentrate. Now the balance in riding is compounded when someone else is riding with you. You don't know when they're going to move or look around as they sit behind you. But when they move, you are plenty conscious of it because you immediately have to compensate and balance the motorcycle.

Another added challenge in riding a motorcycle is: it takes both hands and feet to coordinate the ride. Your left hand controls the clutch, lights, and turn signals, plus steering. Your right hand controls the front brakes, horn, starter, off-on switch, and steering. Your left foot controls the gear shift. Your right foot controls the back brakes.

Also, when you are riding, you never know what the traffic around you will do. Most of the time, the drivers of other vehicles see you and all goes well, but there is always that driver who doesn't see you. So you concentrate and learn to ride a motorcycle defensively.

Now you begin to understand that it takes keen concentration to ride a motorcycle. You have to forget virtually everything else, and you have to think in another area of your brain, thus giving a rest to that part of your mind which has been under stress.

Some people find this type of diversion in golf, fishing, boating, and other areas of activity. This is why it is healthy for people to have hobbies or other active outlets.

Dear Christian friend, it is OK to play, rest, and relax. It is necessary and recommended for the wholeness which you should feel as a follower of Jesus Christ.

If you run at full speed in only one area of your life, you will soon crash. Like a freight train going down the track, you pick up speed and sometimes are not aware of how fast you are going. On the straightway you can get by with the speed, but up the road somewhere there will be a curve. It is generally the "curves" in life that throw us.

When driving down the highway, occasionally you will see a sign in reference to the fifty-five-miles-per-hour speed limit: "Slow down and live!" This may be applied to Christian leadership. Don't try to do everything yourself—involve others. It is a good idea to keep in mind that the secret to success is involvement. Learn to involve other people. Enlist others to carry the load and share the success with you.

See a doctor for a thorough physical. You may need

some vitamins. You may need to eat balanced meals. This is a simple matter, but necessary for positive leadership.

Now that we have thought about the physical side of your life, let's move to another aspect of the well-rounded church leader.

Learn to accept yourself. Some people are always putting themselves down as inadequate for one reason or another—always wishing they were like someone else. God made you the way you are for a purpose. Accept the physical way you are, unless is is something definite you can do about it. If you are overweight or underweight, you can change that. Make this a spiritual, as well as a physical, goal. Remember the verse, "I can do all things" (Phil. 4:13).

Recently I was leading a meeting and was preaching on the theme of living positively as a Christian. I asserted, "You can do whatever you want to do if you want to do it badly enough." I also explained that God intended everyone who was saved to serve, not sit. Regardless of your physical condition, you can do something for the Lord.

I presented numerous ways people could serve in outreach visitation, such as knocking on doors, using the telephone, picking up people for church and Sunday School, contacting people on the street, etc. At the invitation time of dedication for service, many people walked down the aisle. One man couldn't walk—he was in a wheelchair. He wheeled himself down the center aisle, stating he wanted to serve the Lord in visitation outreach. His testimony was, "You showed me a way to use the telephone, write postcards and letters, and see people on the street." Then he wheeled himself back up the aisle. Here was a man who was literally "letting his fingers do the walking" in contact-visitation. He had no legs.

Accept your physical condition. Change what you can.

Then ask God to show you ways and means of doing what you want to do for Him.

Family and Home

Many religious leaders become caught up in their "calling" to their work. They need to keep in mind that God has also given a high priority to family and home.

Do you make time for your family? Are certain days family ones? Are certain hours of the day reserved for the family? There are several approaches to scheduling family time.

Too many times, our families receive the "leftovers"—time left over after we have done everything else. Then, because of fatigue, the leader has drained most of his energy that could produce happiness. Or when family time finally arrives, it is all used up doing household chores, such as mowing grass, fixing a door, cleaning the garage, sweeping the patio—on and on goes the list. Thus, no happy family time occurs.

Do you have some home goals? Dreams such as building a home, painting a house, planning for retirement? Do you initiate vacation plans with the family about where they would like to go and what they would like to do? How long would they would like to stay? It is a part of important training and leadership for children to be given input about locations, time, and activities for a family vacation.

My youngest son, Jonathan, decided he wanted to go to Disneyworld for a weekend. My wife and I let him make the decisions about where to eat, where to stay (anywhere with a swimming pool), what to see, what to do, rides to take, and how long to stay.

It was a tremendous weekend for him. We ate mostly at McDonalds (not exactly my style). We rode crazy rides which kept me on the dizzy side most of the day. We spent the rest of the time in a nearby motel swimming pool. All of these activities were his choices.

My oldest son, David, also had his week when he called the shots. At the end of the time, he declared, "Boy, Dad, didn't *we* have fun?" This made it all worthwhile.

My daughter Karen's "biggy" was for her and her mother to spend a week at Daytona Beach in a motel with nothing to do but eat, sleep, and sun. Her remark was, "Now, that's living!"

In your family and home, what are some goals you need to set and accomplish? These are goals that will be remembered as the good times of life.

I repeat: take time for family and home. Initiate discussions. Write down plans. Put them on a calendar. Set aside money for the activity. Build anticipation with periodic purchase of items to be used or worn during the event.

For some, family time can be accomplished by eating out in good restaurants or going on one-day outings to zoos, parks, lakes, or entertainment centers in your area. Start thinking along those lines by talking to your family about some possibilities. It will amaze you what will come into focus. Remember that the years you have with your children at home will be here and gone, never to be recalled again. Enjoy them, for they will be soon be gone.

Education and Learning

Most people have completed some type of formal education—grade school, high school, college, graduate school, etc. Sometimes holding the certificates or diploma in hand leads the learner to feel he has no further need to learn. Wrong!

The Bible says, "Study to shew thyself approved unto God, a workman that needeth not to be ashamed, rightly dividing the word of truth" (2 Tim. 2:15). The thrust of "study" means "be diligent" or "apply yourself."

A person should never stop reading and attending classes, seminars, and conferences to improve one's skills. All of these activities will help you to be a more effective Christian leader.

Much reading can be done for general information on what is going on around you. A well-read person can carry on a conversation about almost anything. So be sure to read the newspaper and several newsmagazines.

It is smart to read materials in those areas which highly interest you, such as spiritual and religious matters. But it is also wise to know what is happening in other areas of life.

Find out the special interests of your fellow workers, your neighbors, your acquaintances. Read material in their areas of interest so you can ask questions and make conversations. Your education and personal relations will increase because others can expound their knowledge to you when you ask various questions.

Being a good listener enhances learning. If you do all the talking, you may learn practically nothing.

My brother, Dick, is an excellent listener. He has remarked on several occasions, "People think I know more than I really do. I listen and ask a question now and then, and they think I'm a real expert on the subject. Silence with a quizzical look often gives an impression of superabundant wisdom and thought over what is being said. It's amazing how much I learn just by listening."

There's a splendid lesson here for all of us. To learn more, work at being a good listener. Remember, you are not learning anything new if you are doing all the talking.

My desire to know more Scripture recently increased. But, admittedly it's hard to find time to sit down and read the Bible. So I purchased recordings of the New Testament on cassette tapes. It's possible to listen to the entire New Testament in about fourteen hours.

While driving, I slip a tape into the cassette player and listen. I don't concentrate intently or try to grasp all that is being said. I listen in a relaxed mood. When a thought catches my attention, I concentrate on it. It's amazing the amount of information you can gather about the New Testament while listening to it being read.

By using this process, you learn more than you may realize. Scientists and researchers tell us that every sensation of the body is recorded in the mind. That is, all the sounds around you are thus recorded. All your eyes see, both consciously and unconsciously, are recorded. All your body feels, all of the smells and what you taste, are recorded in the brain.

Since this is true, why not allow the mind to be filled with sounds of the Word of God and recorded in the conscious and the subconscious? It will surface at a time needed. God promises, "My word . . . shall not return unto me void" (Isa. 55:11).

Motivational tapes by many different speakers and motivators are plentiful and can be used in the same manner. An example of an excellent motivational tape is *An Effective Visitation Program,* a sixty-minute Broadman tape. Many more are available.

You can learn to do *several things at once.* This is called maximizing your time and energy. Use every possible method to pour knowledge into your mind. This will make you a more effective Christian leader.

Business and Financial

Contrary to popular opinion, religious leaders should be good in money matters. In other words, pay your bills.

Your words of leadership can become as "sounding brass or a tinkling cymbal" if your hearers know you are overextended financially and you have "bad debts" in the community. If you are a bad financial risk, people will question your judgment in spiritual affairs.

Set some goals to correct these problems. If necessary, seek out someone as a financial adviser to help you work out these matters. In some places this service may be provided free. Start by checking with human services, social services, or small business services. These agencies can direct you to someone in your community who can give you help.

This is also a vital service that could be provided by some churches. People in the congregation and community often have financial problems, also. Ask the church leadership if seminars on this subject could be conducted in the church for members, as well as the community at large.

Christian leaders should plan for retirement. Most religious leaders find they must supplement their income in order to provide a secure future. This means finding additional ways to earn extra money.

There are various forms of making extra money. It is the *love* of money that is wrong. I think God wants us to take the "talents" (money) he has given us and compound it. Remember the parable of the talents? (Matt. 25:14-30). The good servant that invested wisely doubled the talents which God gave him. But God took the one talent which the lazy servant had and bestowed it upon the industrious servant. The talent referred to here is not something you can do like sing, play an instrument, or speak. The talent referred to in this parable is money or possessions. Notice that one servant went out and buried his talent. You cannot bury an ability in the ground. Therefore, these talents must refer to actual money. However talents (abilities) like singing, etc., are good, of course, and should be used for God's glory.

It is a wise person who gives 10 percent to the Lord in tithes of what he makes. It is a wiser person who takes an additional 10 percent of his earnings and saves that or invests it to bring glory to God.

A prudent person will also be open to other avenues of making money. Too many times we put blinders on ourselves and prevent ourselves from making extra money.

When I first came to the Baptist Sunday School Board in 1963, I thought because I traveled so much I didn't have the opportunity to make extra money. I also thought any part-time sidelines to make money were out of the question. I felt I was on a fixed income for life. I was dedicated to Christ's cause, and I thought dedicated people shouldn't think about making extra money. Wrong.

A person with whom I became upset challenged me, "Neil, you've put blinders on yourself. This week while you are on the road traveling, open your mind to possibilities for making extra money."

Ridiculous, I thought, *How dumb can that person be?* I had locked myself in by my pattern of thinking. But while driving on that trip, I let my mind wander to possible ways I could make extra money.

I was driving my station wagon through Georgia. I pulled into a little country store in the middle of nowhere for a cold drink. The merchant had several round oak tables for sale at $10 each. I bought what he had and loaded them into the wagon. The next weekend I sold them out of my garage for $50 apiece by placing an ad in the community newspaper.

That started me in the business of using sidelines to make extra money. The "blinders" came off. As I tried one sideline and succeeded, another opened up. I became knowledgeable in antique furniture, cut glass, coins, antique cars, boats, and motorcycles, and finally real estate and rental properties.

If we don't place "blinders" on our eyes, we become sensitized to what is going on around us. When we become aware of money-making opportunities, doors begin to open because of the broadened knowledge which we have gained. It opens areas of conversation that were never before possible. It opens opportunities to witness in a broader sense than simply the written word. You are able to build relationships with people because of your broadened knowledge. Therefore, it is easy to see that you benefit financially, educationally, socially, and in other areas of life when you think about sidelines for making extra money. Therefore, work at taking the "blinders" off.

Many successful Christian leaders I know have a number of profitable sideline interests.

The *key* is to keep the sideline a sideline to your spiritual calling. Don't allow a sideline to obsess you, or you will lose track of your spiritual calling. Only the spiritual calling can give you a rich, fulfilling life.

Set some goals in the business and financial side of your life. Some may be long-range and some may be short-range. Think now about retirement and how you are going to live at age sixty, sixty-five, or seventy when your working years are over.

I have approached the financial aspect of being the "whole" Christian" in order to encourage you to prepare financially for retirement, at whatever your age. It is important for one to prepare one's attitude for retirement. Develop an activity now that you enjoy as a sideline; then it will not be difficult to give more time to this activity after retirement. After retirement it can become a mainline activity which you can control. Then no one can claim that it is time for you to quit or move—or that you are no longer needed.

A preacher with tears in his eyes confessed to me, "Neil, I'm sixty-two. I have had a successful ministry here at this church for a number of years. We have increased in every area of the church, but now my church wants me to move. We have no home. Our savings aren't enough to buy a home, and who wants a sixty-two-year-old preacher?"

It's so sad, at the end of a successful ministry, to suffer the feeling of defeat and rejection.

To have a well-rounded Christian life and a feeling of accomplishment at the end of a successful ministry, plan now that the financial and business sides of your life will be in good order. It is not too soon to start thinking about this. Neither is it too late.

Religious and Spiritual

This part of your life has been deliberately left for the last. We ought to set goals in the religious and spiritual area of our lives. I hope most of us have done this. In previous pages I have emphasized goals of various kinds, how to set them and accomplish them.

If we set and accomplish goals in other areas of life, we are more apt to become better spiritual leaders. Our desire as Christians should be to become the most effective, wholesome Christians possible.

As we set, maintain, and reach goals in other areas of our lives, this strengthens our spiritual leadership. This will enhance our ability to be more effective, wherever God has called us to minister.

Those we lead become more ready to believe our spiritual approach to life as they see us try and sometimes fail in other areas of life, but see us keep on pressing toward the goals we have set.

The depth of your spirituality without you "telling how spiritual" you are or how dedicated you are, *is seen.* It comes through to the listener and follower, for they know you have walked where they have walked—and you have conquered. It becomes more believable when you testify "I can do all things through Christ which strengtheneth me" (Phil. 4:13).

People will become conscious of your dealing with problems, setbacks, near successes in home life, business, education, and physical areas in your own life, and not giving in or giving up. They will be encouraged by your perseverance.

They will see you readjust and go at it again and again until you finally succeed. Many people think it is shallow to *talk* of "spiritual perfection" all the time. Yet, there are many Scripture references which lend themselves to *working constantly or aiming* toward perfection.

- "I press toward the mark" (Phil. 3:14).
- "Forgetting those things which are behind" (Phil. 3:13).
- "Where there is no vision, the people perish" (Prov. 29:18).

Therefore, working toward perfection or success in all areas of our lives and being successful have a greater impact on those we lead spiritually.

Strive toward being a strong, positive, successful, spiritual leader. Set and accomplish goals in other areas of your life—home and family, education and learning, business and finance; physical condition and health. Doing this will make you a stronger church and spiritual leader.

Learn to Listen

Many times people are not motivated because they did not get the message from you. In other words, what you were saying did not "compute." Never assume everyone totally understands what you mean when you use certain words or illustrations.

Here is an acrostic I like. It is called *KISS*.

K

I

S

S

The problem I have with this particular acrostic is the word that is given to the last "s": *keep it simple, stupid!* I do not like the word *stupid,* for practically no one is completely stupid. So I substitute the last "s" to *Keep I t Simple Somehow.* Work at keeping your words, ideas, and illustrations *simple.* I call this the KISS principle.

Napoleon allegedly had an officer on his staff whom he would asked to read the orders of the day for the troops on the front line. The staff officer was not the smartest in the world—in fact, he was kind of dumb. Many people wondered why Napoleon had him on his staff. After handing the officer the orders Napoleon would ask him: "Do you understand what has been written?" If the officer said "yes," Napoleon would send the orders forward. If he said "no," Napoleon would send the orders back to be rewritten until the staff officer understood them.

Napoleon figured if the officer could understand the orders given, so could everybody else in the field. This is an amusing story, and we may laugh at it. However, when we are leading, we must work at keeping our instructions simple so everyone can fully understand. Let me illustrate with a personal story.

When my oldest son, David, was about fourteen years old, at the time I was collecting buffalo nickels, whether or not they had dates. At the time there was a certain acid which you could put where an obliterated date once was. You could watch the date reappear on the coin as the acid worked. But you had to keep in mind that the acid had to be washed off as soon as the date appeared. Otherwise, the acid would continue to eat and again obliterate the date on the coin.

One Saturday afternoon I was in the living room with several rolls of buffalo nickels that I was about to process. I had the acid on the footstool and the coins all laid out, and David walked into the living room with a bowl of ice cream. I looked up and asked: "David, go get me a bowl just like that one—only fill it half full of water." His remark back to me was: "Dad, we don't have any more chocolate." That was my clue if I were listening to what he was saying. But my remark back to him was: "I don't care, I don't want any chocolate anyway. I want a bowl just like that one—only fill it half full of water." I can hear some of you giggling since you know what was about to happen. Well, David went to the kitchen, got the bowl, came back, and said, "Here is your bowl of ice cream, Dad."

I looked up and replied: "David, I didn't want a bowl of ice cream. I wanted a half bowl of water." However, I was quick to say, "Since the ice cream is here, leave it, and I'll eat it." So he went back to the kitchen and got me a half bowl of water. I started processing the nickels with the acid, and after about a half dozen or so I glanced over at the bowl of ice cream, which looked as if it was starting to melt. My son was watching as we observed the dates appear on the coins. I reached over, took the bowl of ice cream, dipped out a big spoonful, put it in my mouth, and much to my amazement it had a watered-down taste.

I said, "David, this ice cream has got water in it." He said, "Dad, that's exactly what you asked for. You said get me a bowl just like that one—only fill it half full of water."

We've laughed many times over that incident. However, it certainly taught me to communicate properly and to listen to everything someone is saying, since watered-down ice cream isn't the best in the world.

Affirmation Motivates

Learn to affirm others. In the affirming of others you will subtly become aware of the affirmation coming back to you from people you have encouraged or congratulated, giving them appreciation on their accomplishments. However, a warning, do not affirm others with the expectation that you will receive an affirmation back. This would be the wrong reason for doing the affirming. It should not be for self-grandisment or accolades.

Don't be afraid to praise other people for their accomplishments. So doing will cause you to be more aware of what they are doing, and you may discover methods that will trigger in your mind ideas to accomplish tasks and solve problems. Another closely connected concept is: Learn to say thank you. It costs so little, but means so much to the person(s) to whom you give this expression. Regardless of how small the act or thought or statement might be, appreciation is a necessary part of motivation.

Once I heard: "It is nice to be important, but it is more important to be nice." That statement has the necessary elements I am attempting to convey. Along with being affirming and saying thank you, be open to ideas and suggestions from other people. As you listen and, in a sense, catalog these ideas in your own mind and understanding, they will work in your mind to help you attain self-established goals in your life.

Learn to Say Thanks

Many people don't do anything because they haven't been asked to, or because we ask but don't request a report or say "thanks" and give recognition. We have become our own worst enemy. The worker develops an attitude reflecting "the leaders really don't care because they never ask what happened" after the task is completed, or "leaders never say thank you or give recognition for what I do." Some leaders reply piously, "They should do it because they love Jesus." Many Christians are still babes in Christ and have not developed the Christian maturity of doing things just because they love the Lord.

Keep in mind that church members are human; they need compliments, recognition, and praise. That's not too much to expect for people who give freely of time, energy, and money. Give a commendation, a thank you—a . . . "Well done, thou good and faithful servant" (Matt. 25:21). A pat on the back goes a long way. Bear in mind how much you yourself need affirmation. Learn to say thank you and give recognition and appreciation. Have an annual workers' appreciation banquet. It motivates greatly, engenders positive attitudes, and develops a close bond with your workers.

Volunteer Armies—Senior Adults/Youth

Allow me to interject an idea about volunteer help. We as church leaders are overlooking an "army" of help by not calling on our senior adults or older Sunday School classes as a "project" to do evangelism outreach through the mails, telephone, census taking, secretarial work, and other avenues.

A pastor would receive tremendous help if from the pulpit he would ask for senior adults (fifty-five and above) or retired people to volunteer one morning a week, with a coffee break and possible luncheon, to help in an "evangelistic outreach mailing." The pastor could have 3 by 5 cards in the bulletin or in the pews, and ask those who would be willing to volunteer for the project to take a card, fill it out, and drop it in the offering plate (see sample).

I Will Volunteer _____

Name _____

Address _____

Phone _____

    (circle one) Mon. Tues., Wed., Thu., Fri.

I need a ride____Yes ____No

Another approach would be for the pastor or minister of education to go to several older adult classes during Sunday School and ask for a class to accept the one-time mailing emphasis as a "class evangelistic outreach project."

The "volunteers" could do the following, depending on the church's office equipment available:

- Make lists of names and addresses for mailing
- Type
- Address
- Fold
- Insert
- Stamp
- Check zip codes

Another large "volunteer" army is the youth.

Youth could meet several hours in the evening, Saturday morning, or Sunday afternoon. Again, emphasize the project as an "evangelistic" one. Again, the pastor is the appropriate person to ask the youth and give them a challenge to take on the task. Let the youth decide when would be the most convenient time to meet when they could have the largest group together.

You have plenty going for you when you approach the task as "evangelistic." I use the word *evangelistic* in the broadest sense.

There may be a degree of reluctance about accepting that concept. However, let me remind you that if a church does not have the names of prospects, it really doesn't matter how many trained evangelistic soul-winners or out-reachers you may have. You cannot do evangelism without prospects. Remember, Paul says, "I have planted, Apollos watered; but God gave the increase" (1 Cor. 3:6).

Everyone is needed to find and help enroll prospects for the Sunday School. People are desperately need to make contacts and to visit. Then the Holy Spirit can work in the prospects' lives so conversion can come about. Everyone who helped get that lost person from where he was to attendance, and eventually down the aisle, accepting Christ, had a part in winning that person to the Lord.

Keep in mind that the secret to success is involvement. The more people involved, the more successful will be your program.

James 4:2 chides us: "Ye have not because, ye ask not." If you fold inserts and stamp envelopes for the glory of the Lord, you have a part in evangelism, for the apostle Paul says, "We are labourers together with God" (1 Cor. 3:9).

Everyone cannot be a preacher, teacher, singer, or public "pray-er." But *everyone* can do something somewhere. We, as ministers/leaders miss the mark by not letting people know they can lick a stamp, fold a sheet, or insert a letter for the glory of God.

Enough of my preaching—now back to the mails. Look in my book *Motivational Ideas for Changing Lives* for four sample letters, a mail-back card, and suggestions for twenty other different types of letters.

Use O.P.M. to Motivate

When leading a conference from time to time I will throw in a shock statement to sharpen attention. "Good leaders use O.P.M." is one of those. Of course, it sounds like "opium."

After a long pause when the audience has heard, "Every leader should use O.P.M. I'll repeat the phrase and say, "That's right, I said *use* O.P.M." It will help you to have greater vision, dream dreams, broaden your imagination, make your senses more alert.

I'm sure you can see that by now I have their undivided attention. The audience is on the edge of their chairs and asking themselves, "Is this guy out of his tree? The very idea making such a suggestion, 'use opium!' "

Then I use the chalkboard or an overhead projector and write:

O

P

M

Several groans will come from the audience. I ask, "What do you think I said? I said O.P.M., but you heard something else. Shame on you! You know how I like acrostics and alliteration. O.P.M. is an acrostic." By now I have their undivided attention.

To get a point, concept, or idea across to motivate people, you need to have their undivided attention. Using a shock statement is effective. "Use O.P.M." is one of mine.

What does O.P.M. mean? Simply:

O—Other
P—People's
M—Minds

To be successful at motivation, you need to employ other people's minds and ask them for ideas, for feelings, and for input. Don't try to think of everything yourself. When people give input they are sharing, "Here is the way I would do that." When they make input they, in a sense, are coming toward a degree of commitment. Their ideas and thoughts will stretch your mind, broaden your thinking, cause your creative juices to flow.

But more than that, their input will cement their support of what you are trying to accomplish. Remember, God's three gifts: time, energy, and resources. Using O.P.M., *other people's minds*, is a marvelous resource. Don't be afraid to use O.P.M. It *will* cause you to have greater vision, dream dreams, open your mind to vistas you never imagined. O.P.M.—*other people's minds*. Philippians 2:5: "Let this mind be in you, which was also in Christ Jesus." Think of the power, strength, and positiveness a Christian can have with the mind of Christ. Ask Christ to fill your mind with ideas, solutions, new approaches toward whatever goal you are trying to accomplish.

Let me stretch your mind toward another meaning of O.P.M.:

O—Other
P—People's
M—Money

People in the banking business and loan companies do this all the time. They really don't have their money to use—they use yours and mine which are in savings.

O—Other
P—Preacher's
M—Messages

I don't believe there is a preacher alive who totally preaches sermons that belong to him. Nearly every sermon is an accumulation of thoughts from other preachers he has read or heard. Nothing is wrong with that process since it many times gives validity to the idea, strengthens it, and certainly broadens the listener's mind. Use *other preachers' messages*.

O—Other
P—People's
M—Mortgages

Real estate brokers are constantly involved in this concept. In this day of creative financing, there is a surprising number of ways to use *Other People's Mortgages* to acquire more property.

O—Other
P—People's
M—Materials

Authors, newspaper people, and other types of writers quote *other people's material* for a multitude of reasons.

O—Other
P—People's
M—Machines

In this day of leasing, it is often more profitable to use *other people's machines*. You can lease virtually anything from A to Z—autos to zeppelins. The advantage is that little or no capital is invested—rental price only. No repairs—that is the domain of the owner. You are always using new or almost-new equipment. The user in many instances can receive a tax write-off. There are many other advantages to using O.P.M., *other people's machines*.

Let your imagination run on the O.P.M. concept. See how many more O.P.M. acrostics you can think of.

Now you see why I encourage leaders to use O.P.M. freely. It will create excitement, involvement, expansion of mind, visions, dreams, and imagination.

Involving other people, is a valuable resource, an untapped reservoir, a wealth beyond realization.

Take time and write the names of people you are close to who could give assistance to your goals. Write names of organizations you are aware of but not closely related to that could be of help to you. Let your mind flow freely —don't think of *detailed ways*. These people or organizations could help, simply bring to awareness of mind— there is a possibility.

Most people haven't trained their minds to think in this direction. An attitude has been, "I must do it all myself if I'm a good leader."

A general may win a war but doesn't do it by himself— he has an army. A business may be successful but the president doesn't do it by himself—he has employees. A pastor who succeeds doesn't do it by himself—he has members.

Your success depends on others. Be aware of them, be kind to them, *use* but never *abuse* them. Give the recognition, the praise, the awards, the accolades when and where necessary.

Remember the old adage, "Vinegar never draws flies— honey always does." Therefore, be sweet—use *Other People's Minds, Money, Motivation, Materials, Mort*gages, *Machines*, and *Messages*.

Use O.P.M. It's powerful!!!

Motivating People to Become Involved

For the sake of emphasis I repeat: God gives us three commodities, "time, energy, and resources." Resources can be considered in two aspects: money (or material possessions) and people. Therefore let's consider the need of and importance of people in issuing in success.

April is an opportune time to think of workers for next year or now. You probably need several workers now.

Many church leaders may have the idea that the creation of new units and enlistment of new workers is done only once a year. A growing, going church is reaching people, winning them to the Lord, and growing a congregation in "grace and in the knowledge of our Lord and Saviour" is working every quarter, or at least twice a year, creating new teaching units and adding new workers to the Sunday School.

For example, if your Sunday School has 100 enrolled you should have at least 10 workers or a 1 to 10 ratio of workers (one worker for every 10 enrolled). If this is your ratio, you are in an average or maintenance stance.

A growth stance is one worker for every 6 to 8 enrolled. A decline stance is one worker for every twelve or more enrolled.

As you look at the total Sunday School, it is easy to see quickly how many workers you need to grow a Sunday School. Or, to put it differently it is easy to see how many more workers you need to reach people for Christ and help them grow in the grace and knowledge of the Lord Jesus Christ.

If your church has 500 enrolled and has 50 workers, this is a 1 to 10 worker-pupil ratio. You are in an average or maintenance stance. To grow and reach more people, you must add more workers until there is a ratio of about one worker for every 6 to 8 on roll. To have a 1 to 8 ratio, 63 workers are needed. How did I arrive at that number? I divided 8 into 500, and that gave me 62.5 or 63 workers needed. If I were working toward a 1 to 7 worker ratio I would divide 7 into 500, and I would know that we needed 71 workers. If it were a 1 to 6 ratio, I would divide 6 into 500 and would need 83 workers.

It is a constant task to keep the worker ratio below 1 to 10 in order to keep a growth stance and grow a Sunday School rapidly.

All of these must continue to happen:

- a constant enlistment of workers
- a continuous worker training program
- a continual creation of new units
- a continuous search for potential workers
- a cultivation of mind-set for adult teachers to produce and provide names of possible workers and suggested areas in Sunday School for which they might be suited
- considerable prayer for all of the above, asking for wisdom and guidance in every move you make to enlist workers
- constant search for additional space for members to meet with a new unit

Who Is a Worker?

When figuring the total number of workers in a Sunday School the following positions are those you count.

- All general officers
- All department workers
- All preschool/children's workers
- All youth/adult teachers
- All outreach leaders

- Group leaders (optional about inclusion)

Positions not counted:

- Pianist
- Song leader
- Secretaries
- Assistant/substitute workers
- Class officer positions (president, social chairman, etc.)

What if the worker ratio is way out of line? Let's assume the above was done and you discovered the ratio a 1 to 16 or higher.

Author's note: Some churches I have worked with have had as high as a 1 to 24 ratio, so don't be too surprised or discouraged if you come up with a high ratio. It can be corrected and realigned.

Step 1:

The first step toward correcting the ratio is to discover where the needs. Ask the following questions:

- Does every department have an outreach leader?
- Does every adult Sunday School class have an outreach leader?
- Does every preschool/children's department have the right worker/pupil ratio?
- Does every youth/adult class have the right worker/pupil ratio?
- Are all the department and general officer positions filled?

Step 2:

Make a list of places where additional workers should be added and/or where vacancies exist.

Warning: Don't try to bring the worker ratio from a

declining position of 1 to 16 to a 1 to 8 position in one quarter. It will destroy you as a leader and create immediate problems. Plan at least a year or more to move to the 1 to 8 ratio.

Remember that this whole approach is an educational process. You didn't get a high school or college diploma overnight. It required time.

The "healthy" approach is to fill vacancies each quarter, create a new unit or two, and add several new workers. Remember, move with the people. Don't run off from them.

Step 3:

Decide where you need to create new teaching units. In preschool or children's age groups, a department is a teaching unit. In youth and adult age groups a class is a teaching unit.

Outside the regular Sunday School, the Homebound department is one teaching unit, and the Cradle Roll department is a teaching unit.

Step 4:

Now that the number of new units and the number of workers needed for each unit have been decided, begin making a list of potential workers.

Here is a method for finding workers that will not only give you a list for your Sunday School needs, but will also supply a list for other organizations and committees as well.

When seeking workers most churches make the mistake of looking to adult classes to find them. A number of barriers erected by nominating committees eliminate much good leadership.

Several barriers might be: "How faithful is this person in attendance?" "Are they tithers?" "How much training do they have?" "We need a worker of a particular age." and the barriers continue on and on.

Potential workers should be discovered by looking at the church roll, not just the adult Sunday School roll. Unless the church roll is considered, you will lose sight of many people who have been workers in the past and have quit coming to Sunday School because of various reasons such as a lack of involvement or challenge or some other legitimate reason.

Many people attend the worship services but not Sunday School. Yes, they should be considered as potential workers.

A fact difficult to believe is: if your church is over ten years old, probably over 50 percent of your resident membership is not enrolled in Sunday School. About 90 percent of that group are adults. They are your potential, unchallenged leadership.

It is no wonder 20 percent of the congregation is carrying over 80 percent of the church load. We have not asked 50 percent of the church members to become involved.

"Ye have not, because ye ask not" (Jas. 4:2). Therefore, take the entire church roll. Name by name, ask two questions. First, could this person do a job in our church if they would agree to? Do not think of a particular job, since you are preparing a list of potential workers only, not considering specific places of service.

If you can say yes to the above question, then ask the second. Would the church accept this person as a worker?

If you can answer yes to this question, you may have have found yourself a potential worker. Put that person's name on the list of potential workers.

Most nominating committees want a worker to be "perfect" before being considered. Those committee members forget where they were in their church life when the Lord found them. We also forget how Christ has had patience, love, and understanding to move us from where we were to where we are now. We are still a "far piece" from being perfect. Let's be aware of the leadership of the Holy Spirit in guiding us to people. Let's trust Him to help us develop them.

You will soon have a list of potential workers, longer than you may have thought possible.

Training and Guidance Motivate

Once you have gone through the entire church roll, (notice you picked up those enrolled in the adult classes) you now have a large list of potential workers. Now you are ready to make several approaches to enlisting and training, depending on what you want to accomplish.

Motivational Option 1—You are needing workers for a particular age group.

Step 1—Pray through the Holy Spirit and ask, "Lord, who on this list should we consider to work with this age group?" One by one look at every name and consider the person mentally, emotionally spiritually, physically, educationally.

Step 2—When an impression (leadership of the Holy Spirit) hits you as you look at the name, write it on the list for the particular age group.

Step 3—You have gone through the entire potential worker list, considering each name. You now have a list of potential workers for a particular age group.

Step 4—Enlisting these people for a worker-training class should be done using a one-on-one method of approach. Your conversation with that person would be as follows:

"Mr. Smith, we feel impressed of the Lord to ask you to be involved in a worker-training class for ———— weeks

(length of time should be given). We meet on ———
(specify time and place—many meet on Sunday morning
or night or on Wednesday night). We believe you can be
used of the Lord in a mighty way of service to this age
group. We want to help you be prepared. Will you do what
the Lord wants you to do?"

Adapt the above conversation to your own style. But
pitch the enlistment on a spiritual level and a "you-are-
chosen" level, not on an "anybody-can-do-it" level, which
is a low motivational level.

Motivational Option 2—Smaller churches needing only
one or two new workers for each age group would not
enlist workers for a particular age group to attend a class
but would merely enlist people to consider being workers
somewhere in the Sunday School. You would still use the
same process as above with a slight change. Encourage the
prospective worker to study the book for a particular age
group by home study.

Motivational Option 3—Use the list for other worker
needs such as Church Training, WMU, Brotherhood, music, outreach leaders, pianists, secretaries, department directors, Sunday morning greeters, and so forth. Any place
of service in your church you have a need, You now have
a readymade source to draw on.

Step 5—Establish a training program using "Guiding"
books of the Sunday School. Begin the training as soon as
you have three or more potential workers. Remember you
are not striving to have a large class. The training classes
may last only six to eight weeks but start a new class each
quarter.

Set the most convenient time for the classes, whether
Sunday morning, Sunday night, Wednesday night, or another time. Have the class when it is most convenient for
the potential workers and teachers.

Step 6—Begin now to build into the adult leadership some of the following concepts.

• The proof of good teaching is not necessarily how large the class becomes. The proof of good teaching is how many times you have multiplied yourself by leading class members out of your class to a place of service somewhere in the church.

What all does this statement mean? Among other benefits, it means every time a person comes out of a class to be a worker or teacher, they probably pattern their teaching after someone. Who is that someone? The majority of new workers pattern their methodology and teaching pattern after the person they have been sitting under as a pupil. Good or bad, the new worker teaches from the "known." The "known" is what they have been watching and learning from you as a teacher for a period of time.

Therefore, when people come out of a class to be a worker, the teacher of the class has helped multiply himself by the number of people that went out. One year I had fifteen people leave my class to go out as workers. Can you imagine having fifteen Neil Jacksons in your church? Oh, oh! It about drove them nuts. The point of the telling? The areas these new workers served increased enrollment by 120 in twelve months. In all probability, Neil Jackson by himself could never have increased the enrollment by 120. Involvement of more people motivates greater participation and fosters growth.

• Build the concept: "You are saved to serve, not sit." Everyone can do something somewhere. Lead people to places of opportunity and growth.

We as leaders need to create places of service for people. Stop asking the same person to do five different jobs in the church. When a person has so many jobs, they more than likely do none of them well, and they soon "burn out." This leaves the church in a difficult situation and sometimes the total loss of the "burned out" person.

• "The secret to success is involvement." The more people you have involved, the more successful your church will be.

• "These have gone out to serve." Make a sign of poster board or a plaque listing the names of class members who have gone out of the class to serve in some capacity elsewhere in the church. List what they are doing and where. This may be called an honor roll.

This method of the service plaque can be a motivator for class members to be involved in some service of the church. It motivates a teacher to develop a mind-set for supplying workers. It is a reminder for the class when a fellowship activity is planned not to forget former class members who are in service. It builds the teacher's self-esteem as a supplier of workers to the total church program. Recognition pays off.

Growth Ideas for a New Year

Up

Periodically there is the need to plan ahead. It becomes a time when the activity itself will motivate people with renewed vision, fresh input, and creative excitement to accomplish great and mighty things.

The time of the year this is done will vary from church to church. Some churches may do this in September, some in January, or some other time of the year. You decide when that time should be. A good Scripture as a basis for planning may be the following: "And seeing the multitudes, he went up into a mountain, and when he was set; his disciples came unto him: And he opened his mouth and taught them" (Matt. 5:1-2). The verses that follow are called "The Beatitudes." Basically, it is the way to be "up" in life. Being "up" is a positive attitude that a person can control. Be "up" in the next Sunday School and/or church year.

- *up* in enrollment of all organizations
- *up* in attendance
- *up* in contacts
- *up* in total teaching units
- *up* in workers
- *up* in training awards
- *up* in number of prospects on file
- *up* in worship attendance
- *up* in baptisms
- *up* in offerings
- *up* in Bible distribution
- *up* in cleanup.

A Dozen Ways for Success in the Upcoming Year

In John 4:35, Jesus saw the "fields" (prospects) and they were "white already to harvest." Many people were ready to hear the good news, to receive the gospel in the simplest form. The multitudes were weary with the world of oppression and depression.

Our nation today is also open to the gospel. Churches that are "up" on an aggressive goal-oriented program of outreach are "reaping the harvest." Resistance to the gospel and the church is the lowest I have seen in the twenty years I've been at the Sunday School Board. It still takes work to reach people, but the returns are worth the effort.

Notice in the Sermon on the Mount that Jesus went *up* into the mountains. The mountains are a higher place. It requires work and extra effort to climb a mountain. As I explained early in this book, it is a place for a selected few; the air is cleaner and purer; the vision is greater and broader. And in the Christian life, the fellowship with Jesus is higher and holier.

Therefore, leading a congregation to a closer relationship with the Lord requires a planning time.

To accomplish this task, the paid staff, the Sunday School Council, and the Church Council need to meet and discuss the needs for the coming year.

You may say, "My church doesn't have a Sunday School Council and/or Church Council." That might be one of the goals for next year—begin these.

If you are the only person (pastor or Sunday School director perhaps) reading this and thinking *we should do something,* then read on. The help that follows will motivate more people. In a sense, the pastor and Sunday School director can make up the Sunday School Council.

1. The first order should be to look over the list mentioned earlier. Pick out those "ups" which you feel are needed in your church. Add others that are needed.

Bring together other leaders (representatives of adult, youth, children, and preschool areas) to talk about the various "ups" that should be considered.

Once this is decided, suggest a date and time that could be set aside. An excellent time is the latter part of September when other workers and potential workers would meet together to plan, prepare, train, and become involved. The more people you have involved in planning Sunday School work, the more successful your program will be.

Looking at the "Ups"

In all the "ups" in which you plan to lead your Sunday School, *do not* set all the goals yourself and report to the people, with your chest proudly thrust out, "Folks, these are our goals." People may say, "Those are *your* ideas and goals. They're *not ours,* so go to it. I feel no real responsibility for these goals. They are *yours.*" They may not say that out loud, but they will probably be thinking.

Learn to involve and trust the people. Lead them to think possibilities. Let them decide and voice the challenge. Remember when people verbalize and have input, they have committed themselves to the project. When workers are allowed to think, decide, and verbalize, they often come up with higher goals than would have been set for them.

Do not read into the above that I am saying, *Don't have goals, ideas, or visions in your mind before you go before the people.* You need to have certain goals so people will be assured that *you know* where to go or what to attempt. You must also project the fact that their help is needed in attaining the goal.

Let's look at each of the "ups" mentioned above.

• *Up the Enrollment*

It has been proven through the years; when Sunday School enrollment goes up, so does the attendance. Lead *each* department and class to set an enrollment increase goal. Use a numerical goal, not a percentage increase. It is too difficult to translate, identify, and promote a percentage goal. It is easier for people to understand a number.

Not only should each class or department be led to set a numerical goal, but they should be led to set the goal on a quarterly basis. For example, you may ask, "Could you increase your class enrollment one in the next thirteen weeks?" This makes the goal and responsibility specific, measurable, attainable, rewarding, and within a short period of time. It is difficult to think in terms of one year.

The time frame is vital to success. A person may set a

goal for a year. But like most of us, he will not concern himself until the end of the year, and then the goal generally looks impossible.

Many methods of increasing the Sunday School enrollment can be found in *Motivational Ideas for Changing Lives*.

* *"Up" the Contacts*

Broaden the base of contacting. Emphasize all four types of contacting—door knocking, telephone, cards, and C.C.C. (constant contact consciousness). Encourage the concept of making contacts twenty-four hours a day, seven days a week, not merely a certain night of the week for two hours. Wherever and whenever you see people, invite and remind them of Sunday School.

Increase the contacts and watch the increase in attendance.

* *"Up" the Teaching Units*

For every new teaching unit—a class or department you create—your enrollment will increase about twenty, and attendance will go up about ten to twelve in the next twelve months. Again, back to the enrollment. If you want to increase by 100, you need to create five new teaching units.

* *"Up" the Workers*

For every ten people enrolled, you need a worker. If the enrollment goal is 100, you need at least ten new workers, probably twelve. You may not have enough workers in your Sunday School now. An easy way to find out if you have enough workers is to divide your present enrollment by ten. That tells you quickly how many workers you need. Count the number you presently have. Are there enough?

* *"Up" the Training*

Ideally, at least 50 percent of your workers should have

special leadership training by the end of the year. Therefore, consider calendaring the study of leadership training books that each of your workers needs.

- *"Up" the Prospect File*

A prospect file in a growing church should equal the Sunday School enrollment. This task is more difficult to accomplish in an active church than any other job. You may want to elect a person as the "Director of Prospecting" for the general officers of the Sunday School. When you enroll a prospect, it takes two prospects to replace the one you enrolled from the prospect file. Keep in mind, if you had 100 people enrolled and 100 on the prospect file and you enrolled one of the prospects, you now have ninety-nine prospects but you have 101 enrolled. Therefore, you need to find *two* more prospects to keep this in balance with your enrollment. Now you see why this is a difficult task.

- *"Up" the Worship Attendance*

When the Sunday School increases in attendance, worship services usually do also. Lead workers to encourage the members of Sunday School to stay for worship. Ask the ushers to take a head count. Keep a record for a number of weeks to know more accurately what the preaching attendance is.

- *"Up" the Baptisms*

Another "known" is: for every two lost people we enroll in Sunday School within twelve months, one will accept the Lord. Pastor, do you have a baptism goal? Ask yourself, *How many would I like to see accept the Lord?* If you have no goal or number in mind, you probably will not perform many baptisms.

To lead one person to the Lord each week would give you fifty in a year, with two weeks off for vacation. Quite a record when you consider that more than 6,000 of our

37,000-plus Southern Baptist churches and missions last year did not baptize *one* person in twelve months! Have a baptism goal.

• *"Up" the Offerings*

When people come, they give. This means more money for God's work—more money for missions, materials, and ministry.

• *"Up" Bible Distribution*

Holman Bible Publishers of the Baptist Sunday School Board has produced a New Testament which can be bought for thiry-two cents a copy in quantities of fifty or more. Contact the Baptist Book Store for more information. One of the best ways to find prospects is to sponsor a community Bible distribution on the theme, "The Word of God in Every Home." Giving someone a New Testament opens the door to all kinds of opportunities for witnessing.

• *"Up" the Cleanup*

In many churches one of the best activities to begin a year is to have a workday at the church. You can involve many people in such an activity. Take down all outdated posters, clean out cabinets, get rid or fix broken furniture, empty storage rooms, and provide space for people. God called a church to save people—not to accumulate junk. Sweep up, paint up, fix up, wash up, dust up, pick up, set up, light up, clean up, and brighten up. Straighten up the whole church. All will be lifted up by the attitudes, smiles, and attentiveness of the congregation on the Sunday after a work day like this.

Many people are actually waiting to be asked to help. Maybe they cannot teach, sing, preach, play an instrument, or pray in public (the five things we as church leaders "seem" to think are the most important jobs). We must involve more people in other activities of service. There is no insignificant service for Jesus.

Plan an "up" time and have tremendous preparation for the new church year.

Motivate the Evangelism Team

"And he gave some, apostles, and some, prophets; and some, evangelists and some, pastors and teachers" (Eph. 4:11). Some translations use the phrase "varied gifts of the ministry."

To me this verse of Scripture projects the concept that all people can do something.

Some churches have the attitude that if you can't preach, teach, sing, play an instrument, or pray in public you aren't much." And that's not how God feels about it.

This attitude needs to be squelched and destroyed, for it is untrue and not Scripturally based. Looking again at Ephesians 4:11, the concept is for every person to find a place of service which they can joyfully perform to the fullest of their abilities.

Having this in mind, let's think about various aspects of reaching people.

Five concepts need to be considered for a church to grow. These are not in any descending order of importance.

- Soul-winners
- Enrollers
- Prospectors
- Contacters of Absentees
- Pray-ers

These are five major areas of an outreach ministry. According to the concept expressed in Ephesians 4:11, there is a need to emphasize all of these. We must make people aware of the emphasis, and we need to help them find their areas of service according to their gifts in personality, ability, emotions, and desires. If possible they need to choose the area for which they are best suited. We have a responsibility to help them maximize their ability for evangelism/outreach.

Allow me to expand on each area for better understanding. The first group of people are the soul-winners.

Soul-Winners

Soul-winning is the ultimate goal of the Scriptures, for it presents the entrance into heaven where a person accepts Christ as Savior. It is imperative to develop a group of people to do soul-winning. There is a group in every church that is capable of soul-winning. This small group needs to be sought out, challenged, and trained. Of course, there may be the need to change the mind-set of the congregation.

Negative attitudes and excuses about soul-winning exist in most every congregation. Here are a few:

- "Soul-winning is the pastor's job or some of the paid staff."
- "We who are soul-winners are the only ones doing anything of any consequence in the church."
- "Unless you are a soul-winner, you're not doing evangelism."
- "I need to know 100 Scripture verses before I can do evangelism."

Many more alibis are prevalent. Each of these statements have an element of truth but are not totally true. They are negative in thinking. However when the congregation becomes aware that only a small group for soul-winning is sought after, their mind-set soon changes. In the past ten years I have yet to find a church with even

5 percent of its congregation actively winning people to the Lord.

Many churches are doing an excellent job of training their congregation in soul-winning with such programs as CWT, WIN, EE, etc. These splendid programs are needed.

One problem, however, lies in the fact that most churches do not have many lost people coming to their services. Their prospect list for evangelism is miniscule.

After a soul-winning emphasis such as those mentioned above, most all soul-winning prospects enrolled in Sunday School or attending the worship services are won to Christ in a short period of time, and the soul-winning program slows down or grinds to a halt.

A constant flow of lost people enrolled in Sunday School being nurtured as soul-winning prospects is the need. In a sense, preparation for salvation is an educational process, occurring as the prospects hear the Word of God. Hearing the Word through preaching and teaching convicts the prospect to receive Christ when and where the Holy Spirit has a chance to work.

The non-Christian needs to learn the meaning of the words *lost, saved,* and *born again.* It is no wonder that Nicodemus in John 3 asked Jesus: "How can a man be born when he is old? can he enter the second time into his mother's womb?" (vv. 4-5). Jesus was using words that Nicodemus did not understand. He asked for clarification of Jesus' words. Therefore, an educational process is needed.

With this in mind you can quickly see that an emphasis on enrolling lost people in Sunday School is necessary if your church continues to grow and minister in your community.

The most likely person to head up the soul-winning

group is the pastor. The next group of people is the enrollers.

Enrollers

Enrolling people in the Sunday School is a vital part of reaching people. I feel that the most important figure in your church is its Sunday School enrollment. From that you may draw people for all other programs of the church.

If the Church Training program is to grow, it must find its prospects from the Sunday School roll. If the music program is to grow, it must do the same.

If the mission organizations are to grow, they have to do the same.

If a stewardship program is to be successful, it needs to be worked through the Sunday School.

If a church is to increase in baptisms, it must work at enrolling lost people so they can hear the Word of God before they believe.

Here is a shocking estimate: If we go down the street knocking on doors to present the plan of salvation, we would need to knock on 240 doors and present the plan of salvation 240 times before winning one person to the Lord!

Yet, you have heard that if you enroll three people in Sunday School, in twelve months you will win at least one to the Lord.

Recently Andy Anderson, a growth specialist at the Baptist Sunday School Board, did a critical study of 285 churches that are on "The Growth Spiral." The Growth Spiral is a concept and methodology he developed to help churches increase their congregations. These churches participate on a volunteer basis and are not selected by the denomination. Any church that chooses can participate by contacting Andy at the Baptist Sunday School Board.

He presented these facts of success and findings in what is called "The White Paper."

Of these growth-minded 285 churches, it was discovered that for every two lost people enrolled in Sunday School, they would win one to the Lord in twelve months. This should be fabulous news and encouragement to churches that want to become aggressive in reaching people.

It is evident from the above that if a church wants to have 100 baptisms, it needs to enroll at least 200 lost people in Sunday School.

The most likely person to head up those who enroll people in the Sunday School is the Sunday School director. He wants to see the numbers increase. That is his responsibility. It would be wise to develop a team of workers that concentrate on enrolling people. This group could once a quarter make a special effort of enrolling people on a given Sunday afternoon. The people in this group should have the gift of enrolling people. Many of these people will be salespersons. They have learned the skill of getting a person's name on the dotted line.

Some "pious" person may want to protest, "All you are interested in is numbers." And you can softly and spiritually reply, "That's right. For the numbers are names and the names are people." Without people we have no ministry, no fulfilling of the Great Commission, no crown of righteousness for His glory. Numbers are needed!

The next group of people is the prospectors.

Prospectors

These are vitally necessary to a growing church. Without them, the enrollers would soon run out of prospects to enroll, much like those who are soul-winners running out of lost people enrolled in Sunday School.

There is a constant need to find prospects for the Sunday School. It would be great to have a group of people who are the prospectors. Consider electing a general officer as director of prospecting. The group of prospectors are in a constant mind-set to find prospects. That becomes their ministry—to find prospects to give to the enrollers to enroll.

Remember: PF = SS ENR. What that means is "prospect file equals the Sunday School roll."

My book, *Motivational Ideas for Changing Lives,* has a number of ways to find prospects.

The prospector would periodically do an area-wide people search—go down the streets knocking on doors asking people if they are *attending* church anywhere. If not, they fill out a People Search Family Card (4333-40) for the entire family. Contact the Baptist Book Store for this card.

Many people in the church have no qualms about going down the street taking a survey and gathering information. But don't ask the same persons to do soul-winning, since they have deep fear about this activity. Some of those people have problems in simple absentee visitation or enrolling people. They feel inadequate to do soul-winning or any other type of outreach emphasis, but it does not bother them to take a survey on a Saturday or Sunday afternoon.

The most likely person to be responsible for this periodic emphasis would be the minister of education, if the church has one. He would head up the making of maps, enlisting those prospectors, and on a given Sunday afternoon, probably the last Sunday of the quarter, would initiate the action of going out and discovering new prospects. The prospectors would continue to use any other method of finding prospects for the Sunday School through the rest of the quarter. If your church does not have a minister of education, it would be the responsibility of the Sunday School director to head up the prospecting. Or, as was suggested, elect a general officer that is the director of prospecting.

I mention periodic. By this I mean every three to six months, do a people search in an area of your church field.

It is possible to have an ongoing people search by employing those who volunteer to give several hours a week, any day of the week, any time of the week they choose to knock on doors. There is in every church an untapped resource of people available to do this task.

Consider people who are retired and older high school youth. Use them on a Saturday or Sunday afternoon.

The *Prospectors* are continually working at keeping the prospect file equal to or more than the Sunday School enrollment. Remember when the enroller enrolls one person, the prospectors have to find two prospects.

Remember that it takes change to grow. The greatest change is that of mind-set. If you are going to grow, you must want to grow. And wanting to grow will require some changes of minds, attitudes, policies, procedures, and people. An "I-can-do" attitude needs to develop. Now, the next needed group is the contacters.

Contacters of Absentees

A fourth group of people involved in evangelism/outreach team are the contacters of absentees.

These are members of the class who do not have any reservation or apprehensions about contacting someone they know. They feel a closeness to the class members and will make a phone call, drop them a card, or see them. They feel comfortable in this type of activity. Some churches call these people inreachers. I think it is wrong to put people on "guilt trips" because they don't do outreach. Help them to find a method they feel comfortable in doing. Then encourage them to take part in that form of service. Remember, everyone has different abilities. The most likely person to head this group is the outreach director of the Sunday School.

Pray-ers

The last group of people in the evangelism/outreach team are the pray-ers.

"The effectual, fervent prayer of a righteous man availeth much" (Jas. 5:16).

Without prayer we can do nothing effectively. Using all of the above, a spiritual, growing church can be developed.

All of us should pray, of course, but there are some Pray-ers who for some reason cannot do any of the above methods of contacting. Yet, they can pray and have power in prayer. They may be shut-ins, homebounds, and senior adults who cannot walk the streets but can and want to have a part in the church program. They can be enlisted to pray.

Find a person in whom others have confidence and know he/she can pray and that God hears his/her prayers. This is the most likely person to head up the group of pray-ers to carry out a function as has been suggested above. Special prayer lists can be made and given to these people who make up the group of pray-ers.

Too many times we pray only for the sick or those in need. It is a good idea to pray for the lost by name before the soul-winners go out and pray for the lost while the soul-winners are presenting the plan of salvation. Pray for the enrollers as they go. Pray for the prospectors as they go. Having an active group of pray-ers can revolutionize your entire church. Revival and evangelism will result.

The above groups are fairly self-explanatory, except

"frequency emphasis." At least once a quarter an all-out effort to enroll all prospects should be made. This could be the last Sunday afternoon of the quarter, or a whole week's emphasis at the end of the quarter.

The same is true of the prospectors. At least once a quarter an all-out emphasis should be made on prospecting, in addition to whatever ongoing method you may have of finding prospects.

All of the ideas above are workable. Change, adapt, modify to fit you and your church. If the follow through of each group is not done, all is lost.

There is a community in Texas called *Prospect*. It is east of Austin about fifty miles on Highway 696 out near Lexington, Dime Box, and Old Dime Box, Texas. A sign near the highway points to the cemetery—"Prospect Cemetery." If we fail to go after the prospects, in a sense we have sent them to the prospect cemetery.

We need pray-ers for all of the above groups.

Prayer is necessary, and pray-ers are necessary to tap the full resources of God and of His kingdom.

A timetable like the following, which lists the person responsible for the actions discussed above, is necessary for success of the evangelism/outreach team.

I am deeply afraid that many churches have a "prospect cemetery." Don't let this happen to you.

Consider the need of building an evangelism/outreach team with all five teams working together to reach people. "We are laborers together" to reach people.

May we as leaders move away from the idea that one group is more important than the others. May we move away from the idea that if you "don't have the gift" in a certain one of the above areas, you are not much. "We are laborers together" (1 Cor. 3:9).

When a person walks down the aisle of a church, making public his profession of faith in Christ, the prospector (the one discovering the name), the enroller (the one enrolling the person), the contacter of absentees (the Sunday School class contacter): the pray-er (who prayed for the prospect), and the soul-winner (the person who led that person to the Lord) can all make praises unto God and to the Holy Spirit, sharing equally in the conversion of the lost person.

For all had a part. Remember, without a name, a soul-winner wouldn't have a chance. The prospector is important. If there were no enroller, the teacher wouldn't have people to teach. The teacher is important. And if we didn't have prayer, all the actions would be done in vain.

Start now to build an evangelism/outreach team. The secret to success is involvement. The more people you can involve, the more successful your church program will be. To God be the glory!

Evangelism/Outreach Team of the Church

E/O Group	Leader Responsible	Frequency Emphasis
Soul-winners	Pastor	Weekly
Enrollers	Sunday School Director	Ongoing weekly/once a quarter
Prospecters	Minister of Education	Ongoing weekly/once a quarter
Contacters of the Absentees	Outreach Director	Weekly
Pray-ers	Spiritual member	Weekly

PART III.
Motivational Scriptures

Note: The majority of these Scriptures I have used in the book. Others are included as an incentive and inspiration to the reader. The Bible is the greatest motivational book in history. Follow it, under the leadership of the Holy Spirit, as your guidebook, textbook, and salvation book (Ps. 119:11,105; 2 Tim. 3:16-17).

Philippians 4:13—"I can do all things through Christ which strengtheneth me."

Matthew 17:20—"If ye have faith as a grain of mustard seed, ye shall say unto this mountain, Remove hence to yonder place; and it shall remove; and nothing shall be impossible unto you."

Mark 11:23—"That whosoever shall say unto this mountain, be thou removed, and be thou cast into the sea; and shall not doubt in his heart, but shall believe that those things which he saith shall come to pass; he shall have whatsoever he saith."

Luke 17:6—"If ye had faith as a grain of mustard seed, ye might say unto the sycamine tree, Be thou plucked up by the root, and be thou planted in the sea; and it should obey you."

Proverbs 23:7—"For as he thinketh in his heart, so is he. Eat and drink, saith he to thee; but his heart is not with thee."

Matthew 5:3-12—"Blessed are the poor in spirit: for theirs is the kingdom of heaven. Blessed are they that mourn: for they shall be comforted. Blessed are the meek: for they shall inherit the earth. Blessed are they which do hunger and thirst after righteousness: for they shall be filled. Blessed are the merciful: for they shall obtain mercy. Blessed are the pure in heart: for they shall see God. Blessed are the peacemakers: for they shall be called the children of God. Blessed are they which are persecuted for righteousness' sake: for theirs is the kingdom of heaven. Blessed are ye, when men shall revile you, and persecute you, and shall say all manner of evil against you falsely, for my sake. Rejoice, and be exceeding glad: for great is your reward in heaven: for so persecuted they the prophets which were before you."

Philippians 4:11—"Not that I speak in respect of want: for I have learned, in whatsoever state I am, therewith to be content."

Genesis 18:14—"Is any thing too hard for the Lord?"

Luke 1:37—"For with God nothing shall be impossible."

Matthew 5:1—"And seeing the multitudes, he went up into a mountain: and when he was set, his disciples came unto him: . . ."

Philippians 3:13-14—"Brethren, I count not myself to have apprehended: but this one thing I do, forgetting those things which are behind, and reaching forth unto those things which are before, I press toward the mark for the prize of the high calling of God in Christ Jesus."

Psalm 119:11—"Thy word have I hid in mine heart, that I might not sin against thee."

Psalm 119:105—"Thy word is a lamp unto my feet, and a light unto my path."

2 Timothy 3:16-17—"All scripture is given by inspiration of God, and is profitable for doctrine, for reproof, for correction, for instruction in righteousness: That the man of God may be perfect, throughly furnished unto all good works."

Isaiah 26:3—"Thou wilt keep him in perfect peace, whose mind is stayed on thee: because he trusteth in thee."

2 Peter 3:18—"But grow in grace, and in the knowledge of our Lord and Saviour Jesus Christ. To him be glory both now and for ever. Amen."

Colossians 3:2—"Set your affections on things above, not on things on the earth."

Psalm 37:4—"Delight thyself also in the Lord; and he shall give thee the desires of thine heart."

1 Corinthians 15:31—"I protest by your rejoicing which I have in Christ Jesus our Lord, I die daily."

Psalm 118:24—"This is the day which the Lord hath made; we will rejoice and be glad in it."

Proverbs 29:18—"Where there is no vision, the people perish: but he that keepeth the law, happy is he."

Matthew 25:21—"Well done, thou good and faithful servant: thou hast been faithful over a few things, I will make thee ruler over many things: enter thou into the joy of thy Lord."

James 4:17—"Therefore to him that knoweth to do good, and doeth it not, to him it is sin."

Proverbs 22:6—"Train up a child in the way he should go: and when he is old, he will not depart from it."

Mark 6:31—"Come ye yourselves apart unto a desert place, and rest a while: for there were many coming and going, and they had no leisure so much as to eat."

2 Timothy 2:15—"Study to shew thyself approved unto God, a workman that needeth not to be ashamed, rightly dividing the word of truth."

Isaiah 55:11—"So shall my word be that goeth forth out of my mouth: it shall not return unto me void, but it shall accomplish that which I please, and it shall prosper in the thing whereto I sent it."

Ephesians 4:11—"And he gave some, apostles; and some, prophets; and some, evangelists; and some, pastors and teachers."